The Birth of God

THE
BIRTH
OF
GOD

by
OLOV HARTMAN

Translated from the Swedish by
GENE J. LUND

FORTRESS PRESS   PHILADELPHIA

This book is a translation of passages from the following books by Olov Hartman, all published by Verbum, formerly Svenska Kyrkans Diakonistyrelses Bokförlag, Stockholm, Sweden:

> *Natten skulle lysa såsom dagen,* 1951
> *Sasom i en spegel,* 1953
> *Oxens tecken,* 1955
> *Gud i nattens timmar,* 1960
> *Medan synagogföreståndaren väntar,* 1966
> *Den bortträngda himlen,* 1967

COPYRIGHT © 1969 BY FORTRESS PRESS

Library of Congress Catalog Card Number 75–84537

2046C69   Printed in U. S. A.   1–172

Contents

v

CONTENTS

III

LET HIM WHO IS THIRSTY COME

Foreword

Like Easter, Christmas is preceded by a time of preparation. I do not know if the old Swedish name for Advent, *julfastan* (literally, "Christmas Lent"), has any counterpart in other languages, but it is certainly true that the reality referred to in that name has influenced the Advent liturgy in many churches. It is significant that in former days the Gospel for the first Sunday in Advent dealt with the second coming of Christ, as it still does in the Roman Catholic tradition. And it is no accident that John the Baptist, one of the most remarkable ascetics in the Bible, appears as Christ's forerunner in a number of Advent texts. Liturgical colors and melodies speak the same language, and even though abstinence in eating and drinking never achieved the same obligatory character in Advent as in Lent, the contrast between Advent as a time of penitence and Christmas as a festival of joy can indeed be seen in external circumstances. In many countries there have been practical reasons for this, inasmuch as winter supplies were limited and the Christmas festival required an accumulation of foodstuffs that had to hold out for at least four consecutive days.

For many people it is still natural to prepare for Christmas by undergoing Advent devotions in the form of examination and meditation, so that during Christmas itself and Epiphany the full and joyous gospel may shine forth. We are familiar also with long-standing popular customs which accentuate the joyful nature of Christmas, customs like the leaving of a simple gift at one's neighbor's door and then disappearing. The giving of bread and other necessities of life, a custom which in Sweden can be traced back at least to the sixteenth century, was based on social need, and was not simply inspired by the Christmas season itself. That this custom is still observed in some areas is due to the fact that human need also persists. Where Christmas was observed in this manner, as a festival for the hungry, it served as an answer to the gospel which is read and preached during Christmas, as a consequence of the celebration of the Lord's Supper, and as a sign of the certainty that God has come to dwell among us.

For the very heart of the Christmas message is that God has become man. Not man in principle, but Mary's son. God's human destiny is neither theology nor myth. God has become history and has thereby identified himself with those who, according to the prophetic tradition, stand out as the leading personages of history, namely, the poor, the oppressed, "even things that are not." This identification is the same in the Christmas Gospel and in the Gospel for Judgment Sunday: "I was hungry, and you gave me food . . . ."

The judgment motif of Advent extends into the Christmas texts too, though under a different sign. The serious character of Christmas was emphasized at an early date by festivals which are no longer observed in many lands: the second day of Christmas, the day of St. Stephen, Martyr; the third day of Christmas, the day of St. John, Apostle and Evangelist; and the fourth day of Christmas, the day of the Holy Innocents, Martyrs, with its terrible account of the slaughter of the children in Bethlehem. The white festival of Christmas day is followed therefore by three bloodred streaks, a triple testimony with roots in martyrdom and oppression. "For behold, darkness shall cover the earth,/and thick darkness the peoples;/but the Lord will arise upon you,/and his glory will be seen upon you./And nations shall come to your light,/and kings to the brightness of your rising."

This proclamation of God's involvement in our humanness has been nearly forgotten in many places. Instead, Christmas is celebrated as a tinsel-strewn legend: "Many believe that Christmas is just a fairy tale, with teddy bears and Santa Claus bearing his sack of trains and dolls and other toys — and then, too, the baby Jesus." (See "The Ox and the Ass" in this book.) The decadence of Christmas is a widespread phenomenon, and those who make serious preparations for Christmas must wonder how this happened. Let me suggest a number of answers.

In many traditions, Christmas has suffered a serious loss of substance because of the disappearance of holy days. Even where men retain the observance of St. Stephen's day (which in many places attracts fewer worshipers than any other service in the church year) Christmas loses its basis in earthly realities and becomes an island of sentimentality, complete with Christmas trees and bell ringing and "Silent Night," with no bridge to things as they really are.

The celebration of the Lord's Supper during Christmas has also fallen away in many places, and as a result the observance of Christmas has lost concreteness and involvement. Christmas has become something one looks at and listens to, not something to participate in. An experience, not a reponsibility. But above all, the concept of the gospel as a gift of bread is being lost, and consequently its intrinsic connection with the bread questions of this world has been lost too.

Furthermore, the old custom of gift giving has been altered so that now we have a veritable frenzy. And something similar has happened to the traditional Christmas table, whose abundance was once related to the fact that it had to stretch so far. Today Christmas dinner is an excuse for the year's greatest orgy in food and drink, a defiant demonstration of abundance in an affluent society which lives side by side with poverty. There are business districts in the large cities of the "Christian world" that, with their false glitter and immense turnover of money and luxuries, contradict and deny the assertion that God has become the poor man's brother.

In keeping with all of this, Advent too has been changed, from a time of fasting into a Christmas decoration. The Christmas gospel appears on Christmas morning, as on an island, but the falsified Christmas, the Christmas of abundance, expands itself from early December to the middle of January.

The chapters in this book are the fruit of many years of striving to recapture the lost Christmas — or, more properly, the lost gospel. My objective is not to recreate an impressive festival. Christmas as museum is incompatible with Christmas as gospel. The idea of an old-time Christmas — with snow, torches, Christmas feasting, and the prestige of gifts—is in all of its falsehood an important public relations factor for the Christmas of abundance. Moreover, to the degree that Christmas appears as a remnant of the good old customs, it loses its message for our time. No revolution has ever begun in a museum. To rediscover the lost Christmas means, as I see it, to rediscover the strongest of all arguments for a position which was stated as follows in Section V (on worship) at the 1968 Uppsala Assembly of the World Council of Churches: "Our worship as Christians must show that we renounce all forms of racial or class segregation, and our communion with Christ must show that we share our bread with his hungry brothers in the world."

It is natural for me, furthermore, to arrange this volume around some words from the Book of Revelation: *I am the first and the last. I am the root and the offspring of David, the bright morning star. Let him who is thirsty come.* Since the world situation is what it is now, the eschatological dimension of the Christmas gospel must be presented in a completely different way than it was when men believed that the problems of the world would solve themselves and that mankind had an endless amount of time at its disposal.

The first part of this volume is completely given over to Advent texts. This part deals with the world we live in, and fastens attention above all to the prophetic dimension in nature and in history. I do not want to be party to the secularizing of existence. Anyone who thinks he can thereby prevent the worship of the circumstances and the things of the world is mistaken. It is precisely when we say that the world is only world that we surrender ourselves and others to the world as to a capricious idol. There is an alternative to contempt for the world and worship of the world. This is the prophetic proclamation that from Genesis to Revelation tells us that nature and history are filled with signs that proclaim the coming of Christ. "Put off your shoes from your feet, for the place on which you are standing is holy ground." In the Old Testament, these words refer to a certain place, surrounding a burning bush. In the life of Christ, they refer to every square yard of earth. Advent lifts us out of the habit of looking upon men and the earth as raw material, and commands us to respect all things and all beings, inasmuch as Christ is the Word from the beginning, and "without him was not anything made that was made."

Another group of Advent texts proclaim that he who was first is also the last. The signs which announced his coming also reveal the goal of history. Human existence is terribly brittle, and we must deal with it carefully. The gospel confirms something that many in our day have discovered with horror: our existence in this world is not eternal. In the gospel, however, this information lacks the quality of desperation that is so often incident to this discovery. History ends, not in meaninglessness, but in a personal relationship. Eternity has a face.

The second major section of this book can be summarized

in the title, *The Birth of God.* I am conscious, naturally, that this phrase could be taken as an argument in the discussion of "the death of God." The fact is that nothing evangelical can be said in connection with talk about God's death apart from the presupposition of his birth. Without this, such talk can only become a diffuse mixture of psychological interpretations of the current age ("God is no longer a living reality to modern man") and of hopelessness concerning the world ("Life is meaningless," or "Nothing is sacred"). Such attitudes have consequences similar to those mentioned above in connection with the secularizing of the world. If the discussion of the death of God includes a gospel of God's impotence, it is presupposed that God has given himself up to such impotence, and even this divine self-giving remains an abstraction, a pale and bloodless idea, if He has not become man. The gospel of God's birth tells us that the signs of Advent, in nature and in history, have been fulfilled and have become flesh.

It is necessary in this context to clean house with respect to the idea of Christmas as legend. In the forward to *The Crucified Answer* (Philadelphia: Fortress Press, 1967) I said that the Gothic crucifix does not say everything about the cross of Christ; the proclamation of its suffering must be completed by the Roman crucifix and its gospel of his divine majesty. The modern Christmas message, it seems to me, must go in the opposite direction. It is truly *God* who has come to dwell among us, but then this is not so hard to imagine — when we are assisted by beautiful music and sentimental art forms. It can be clearly interpreted as saga and myth. But say that God has become *man,* and then it is that the ancient Gnostic contempt for the world is awakened, and it is said that nothing so spiritual could become something so physical. *Finitum non est capax infiniti,* the finite cannot comprehend the infinite. Another version of this answer goes as follows: God's incarnation is blasphemy. How could the highest of all become something so humble? But this is tantamount to saying that the unimportant or the unspiritual or the guilt-laden have no place in God's kingdom. I must admit that there are not many arguments for the gospel which convince me of its truth as strongly as do certain arguments against it, and that what calls forth these counterarguments is certainly not Christmas as myth, but Christmas as a reminder of an historical fact, of a birth which took place here in time and space.

Under the title "I Am the Root and the Offspring of David" the biblical testimony that God appeared as part of a Jewish genealogical table, as a member of a deposed dynasty, and as the son of a certain Mary of Nazareth, is interpreted. God's situation on earth has its roots, however, in human existence itself, even as that existence grows as a plant on the soil of matter — and here the Advent insight about the world returns and is strengthened. And this brings with it certain consequences for our way of observing both ourselves and other men, the earth we dwell upon and the bread we eat. All of the world's segregationists ought properly to forbid the proclamation of the Christmas gospel.

The second part of the middle section, entitled "The Bright Morning Star," is not content to meditate upon the roots of the Christmas gospel in nature and in history; it also falls in worship before "our God in the straw," to borrow a phrase from Luther. If it is true that God became Mary's son, then the ground on which we stand must actually quake. All the sweet Christmas songs are shattered, and a *Sanctus* that shakes the world comes forth. In this context, the responsibility of human life also comes into view: we who have complained that we are in God's power all of a sudden have God in our arms; he is in our power. A playmate of those whom Herod had murdered in Bethlehem, a refugee child, asks us how we can tolerate things as they are in this world.

Someone may ask if I am really in earnest when I take the historical writing of the Evangelists so seriously. Even if Christmas as myth is theologically untenable, is it not the only Christmas one can find? Is not the historical writing of the Evangelists false, from the point of view of scholarship?

In reply I will say first of all that the birth of Christ is not historically indefensible, because his death is an historical fact. In my estimation, it is more important to observe the Evangelists' zeal for establishing the historical basis of the gospel than it is to show that all of their details are in agreement.

In the second place, I will say that I am not a fundamentalist and that my faith will by no means collapse if I cannot bring all of the Bible's chronological details into harmony. I am not even sure that it would be easier for me to believe if the Evangelists had given scholarly lectures using all conceivable documentation. I am suspicious of precise photography, and I prefer Picasso's painting *Guernica* to an exact and detailed description of what actually happened when that city was bombed. As I see it, one comes nearer to reality with the aid of a certain artistic license. The Holy Spirit is not a history professor, he is an artist.

I became convinced of the genuineness of the gospel not as a theologian, properly speaking, but as a dramatist and as a counselor of souls. Human fortunes are as convincing as a load of iron ore. The tormented Joseph, who still agonizes over his wife in his dreams, an introspective man who, precisely because he was such, found his way through the wilderness — he in his solidity is so different from the innocuous old man seen in our crèches. Or consider Mary. The prophets had encountered the angel Gabriel, and they had lost consciousness, they had been so frightened. But Mary did not faint in the presence of this formidable being. After the initial shock had passed, she opened the conversation. She was most certainly endowed with the very kind of bravery required in the one who was to become the mother of the crucified God. In my attempts to wash away the glitter in the pictures of Christmas I also became aware that the reality these people experienced is our own, both in great things and in small. Even the baby's diapers were not forgotten: She "wrapped him in swaddling cloths."

Some of my readers will probably observe that I do not avoid, even so, the Evangelists' belief in miracles, an attitude that conflicts with all of the recognized rules governing that which an historian may accept as reality. If anyone maintained that Napoleon's coming had been foretold by angels, and that he had been conceived without the cooperation of an earthly father, I would not believe that for a moment. But when I encounter such phenomena in the Bible, I yield a bit. What then remains of the assertion that I want to be free of Christmas as myth, in order to get at its real nature?

Let me reply first of all by saying that the Incarnation is the great miracle, and the appearance of angels or a Virgin Birth cannot make it any greater. But if I seek to identify myself with the men of the Bible, somewhat as I do when as a pastor I listen to a fellow human being or when as a dramatist I try to understand my characters, in so doing I find it harder to reject these marvelous events than to accept what is written. By degrees my skepticism finds its way to the other side, and all of a sudden I find that it is doubt which is dogmatic. The familiar discussion concerning Napoleon is in this respect illuminating. There are many Napoleons, but there is only one Christ, and that is the one to whom the Evangelists bore witness. To say that the Incarnation was unique is an understatement. When the Evangelists report, with conspicuous restraint, that this unique event has broken the frame within which "life as usual" is lived, someone will reply that such a thing certainly has not happened since there are no other instances of such an event. But then he is judging the unusual by rules applicable to the universal. At the bottom of this is the preconceived opinion that nothing unique has happened, nor ever will. This is what I call a dogmatic attitude. Much so-called demythologizing is likewise based upon a philosophical viewpoint which, in practice, leaves the field wide open to inexact speech patterns and pretty sentiments. The actual myth here is the Christmas of abundance with the Jesus child in the center, and the only thing that can shake the foundations of this myth is the epic realism of the biblical report.

I said above that Christmas suffers a loss of substance when churches eliminate the Lord's Supper from their Christmas observance. The careful reader will note that a number of the readings in this book presuppose the gospel as *something that happens*. If one wishes to test the reality of the Christmas gospel, he cannot be content just to think about it; he must enter into it. The "church drama" movement has, in many places, revived this method of truth seeking — though the Mass is and remains the center of the reality. (Cf. the Introduction to my *Three Church Dramas* [Philadelphia: Fortress Press, 1966].)

The gospel as event cannot be locked up within a church building, however. Wherever men go, they continue to prove its reality. If the gospel draws us ever deeper into the reality we experience daily, this will be decisive for our confidence in it. In the first part of this volume the questions posed to the gospel by nature and history are accentuated. In the last part, under the title "Let Him Who Is Thirsty Come," the emphasis is placed upon the thirst found in the inner life of all men, and not only in nature and in history. Do all men thirst for the "living water" offered to us in the gospel? This question is not answered on the heights of religious experience or any other. It can be answered only from below. I refer, for example, to such situations — some trivial — as are treated in some of the texts for the post-Christmas season. A young man disappears from home, the wine gives out at a wedding party, someone asks a badly abused woman for a little water.

This volume ends with a reading for Candlemas, the Presentation of Our Lord. In some respects this reading is a summary. "Any one of us can suddenly stand there with a child in his arms — or in his soul. We can suddenly be a brother or a sister to these gentiles or to the man on the outside, suddenly unable to defend ourselves against the realities where God loves."

OLOV HARTMAN

Sigtuna, Sweden
The Presentation of Our Lord, 1969

1. I Am the First

Today

And he came to Nazareth, where he had been brought up; and he went to the synagogue, as his custom was, on the sabbath day. And he stood up to read; and there was given to him the book of the prophet Isaiah. He opened the book and found the place where it was written,

> *"The Spirit of the Lord is upon me,*
> *because he has anointed me to preach good news to the poor.*
> *He has sent me to proclaim release to the captives and recovering of sight to the blind,*
> *to set at liberty those who are oppressed,*
> *to proclaim the acceptable year of the Lord."*

And he closed the book, and gave it back to the attendant, and sat down; and the eyes of all in the synagogue were fixed on him. And he began to say to them, "Today this scripture has been fulfilled in your hearing." And all spoke well of him, and wondered at the gracious words which proceeded out of his mouth; and they said, "Is not this Joseph's son?"

—Luke 4:16–22

The Evangelists Matthew and Mark describe Jesus' visit to the synagogue in Nazareth in connection with incidents which actually occurred much later in his public ministry. Luke, on the other hand, describes this event in his fourth chapter, immediately after Jesus' baptism in the Jordan and the temptations in the wilderness. Clearly this was not done because of deviations in Luke's conception of the chronology of events in the life of Jesus. He chose to use this narrative as a door leading into the gospel, referring particularly to Jesus' remarks concerning the passage from Isaiah: "The Spirit of the Lord is upon me,/because he has anointed me to preach good news to the poor." The Evangelist connects this with what he has just said about Jesus' baptism, when the Spirit of the Lord "descended upon him"; and at the same time he opens up a perspective on the future, anticipating subsequent reports on what Jesus said and did.

Christ was not sent only to Nazareth; it was not only there that he proclaimed the good news. "Today this scripture has been fulfilled in your hearing." This could have been said every day during that "acceptable year" when Jesus went around giving help to all. And, by the same token, this summary of Jesus' preaching has been set as a rubric over the new church year, so that we might know that this is an "acceptable year," a year of grace from the Lord. Thus the First Sunday in Advent provides us with a key to all of the texts that will be discussed during the church year. The fulfillment of the prophetic word concerning Christ is shown in these texts. Here we see the Christ who was sent to preach the good news — or, as the Greek text literally says, "to evangelize for the poor."

But when we use the word "today" to tell us that the sermon preached in Nazareth is pertinent here and now too, we are grappling with an expression which was already questionable that day in Nazareth. For, as far as we can tell, the people who heard Jesus then were convinced that this statement from Isaiah was by no means fulfilled on that day. According to their view, this had already been done in the prophet's own time. And were they not right? Isaiah — or, more properly, the third prophet who speaks in the book of Isaiah — obviously pointed to himself. It was he who was sent to preach liberty to those in captivity, that is, to the Jews held captive in Babylon. These oppressed — or, "ill-treated ones" — constituted a remnant of the people who, in the sixth century B.C., were permitted to return home from the land to which they had been deported. How then could Christ say, "Today this scripture has been fulfilled . . ."?

Let us note first of all that there was a common denominator between the situation in Babylonia and that in Nazareth half a millennium later. In both instances the Jews were subjugated; they did not possess their full freedom. Oppression, captivity, ill treatment are not merely occasional occurrences. We can easily cite instances of these things and date them "today" or "this year." Modern Vietnam and South Africa remind us of ancient Babylon. It is the same world. And so constant are these phenomena — captivity, ill treatment, poverty — that we must interpret them as patterns of conduct that are deeply rooted in humanity, even as we describe a certain animal by saying, "The wolf is a beast of prey."

Yet this is not a fair description of man, at least not according to the Bible. For it is certainly true that when men shackle and torment one another they are giving expression to a tendency common to all men, a pattern inscribed on our very essence. Captivity has its counterpart in an inner situation, in the fact that man is not free. The fact that men mistreat one another is symbolic of the fact that we are all lacerated and broken. But it is precisely here that the Bible stops to remind us that this man is not himself. He was not created thus. His brokenness and lack of freedom have another source. The destructive powers within man have him under their control. He builds prisons because he is a prisoner; as such, he is not himself. For this reason, evil deeds are referred to as "inhuman"; man was not created for this. Christ struck the deepest chords when he spoke of the captive, the blind, the oppressed.

This situation constantly breaks through in history under such slogans as *freedom* for the captive, *sight* for the blind, *release* for the ill-treated. From his particular vantage point the prophet could discern in the political events of his time the first signs of freedom and redress for his people. It is precisely when oppression is relaxed that men begin to see what it means to be rid of it altogether. When men have had some experience with the new state of affairs it is hard for them to *see* freedom and prosperity as a miracle and a gift; we are inclined to take peace and abundance for granted. Thus it is that men can live in the midst of miracles without being aware of them.

But it is not simply our taking things for granted that prevents us from rejoicing over the good days when they come; it is also our realization that they will soon pass away. The freedom the Jews enjoyed did not last long; and what do we know of our own future? The time comes when one questions the appropriateness of rejoicing over conditions that are exceptions to the rule. It is good and well that the sun shines on us, but that does not make it any lighter for those who live in the shadow.

There is a certain amount of agitation in the biblical accounts of delivery from need and of periods of good fortune. The exodus from Egypt, the homecoming from Babylon, the period of independence under the Maccabees — nowhere does the end of the account indicate that the problem has been solved and all is well. When salvation comes, it is looked upon as a reminder of something that was but is not, of a reality which has disappeared. Even though every gleam in the darkness is something of a signal from afar, a harbinger of things to come, it points to something incomplete, a goal not yet reached.

And yet, if we can discern some coherence in the evil things that happen, a negative pattern, we can also see that freedom and well-being are part of a structure, vestiges of the basic structure of life. From an airplane one can sometimes see the lines of an older landscape — overgrown lakes, dried-up brooks, neglected paths, and grazing areas run wild. Thus it is that years of freedom and prosperity stand out as intimations of an original plan, of a way of life that has been abandoned. The prophecies tell us that one day this hidden pattern shall break forth again.

Said Jesus of Isaiah's prophetic gospel: "Today this scripture has been fulfilled." In other words, all of the intimations of the original pattern actually pointed to that day in the synagogue in Nazareth.

The message the prophet was once committed to convey, yes, the role he played in contemporary history, opens up to its fullest depth. All of this is "fulfilled," for Christ has come. The same can be said of the entire prophetic structure that combines Isaiah and his situation with a thousand other signs and events. As a previously unreadable document is deciphered, all of these symbols can now be grouped together in such a way that they make sense. The code is broken, and the mysterious signs can be interpreted. The definitive answer to the question of history has come with deliverance — not deliverance from the Babylonians or from the Romans or from other occasional instruments of power, but deliverance from the destructive principle in life.

The audience in Nazareth first responded with joy at this good news — insofar as they understood it. A long-restrained hope began to spring up. But the report does not end thus. The Evangelist tells us that hope was followed by disappointment. The listeners stopped to ponder this meager fact: There stood a carpenter whom they had known for many years, claiming that the history of the world was fulfilled in him. In this small village, in the midst of an altogether ordinary service of worship. And after thinking it over, they said that nothing had happened. Joy curdled into bitterness.

Jesus was almost put to death then. "But passing through the midst of them he went away," says the Evangelist.

Yes, he went further, first of all to a lunatic in Capernaum, then to one sick with a fever, and later on to many others who were confused about life. We can hear him cry today: "The Spirit of the Lord is upon me,/because he has anointed me to preach good news to the poor./He has sent me to proclaim release to the captives . . . ."

Wherever this gospel goes forth, chains are broken and eyes are opened, just as in the days of the prophets. Yet that is not what is meant by deliverance. Deliverance consists of a personal presence, a presence also felt in captivity, in need, in distress. That is where his travels finally took him — to Gethsemane, to the cross. "The Spirit of the Lord has sent me to evangelize." His gospel also points the way to freedom. It breaks through the pattern of conduct that is otherwise thought to be basic to our nature, the pattern of conduct which characterizes captivity and cruelty. In the gospel a new zone of freedom breaks into the open; here it is that we come into contact with our human origins, with the Christ-dimension. This was true at that Advent service in Nazareth, but it was also true in the prison where John was held, and before the council where Stephen was brought by his executioners. This is true throughout the entire church year, right up to Judgment Sunday. "Today this scripture has been fulfilled." This is a year of grace: a vein of grace runs through the ages, and it is possible for each one of us to find it. Believe the gospel.

Holy Is the Earth

The earth is the Lord's and the fulness thereof,
  the world and those who dwell therein;
for he has founded it upon the seas,
  and established it upon the rivers.

Who shall ascend the hill of the Lord?
  And who shall stand in his holy place?
He who has clean hands and a pure heart,
  who does not lift up his soul to what is false,
  and does not swear deceitfully.
He will receive blessing from the Lord,
  and vindication from the God of his salvation.
Such is the generation of those who seek him,
  who seek the face of the God of Jacob.

Lift up your heads, O gates!
  and be lifted up, O ancient doors!
  that the king of glory may come in.
Who is the King of glory?
  The Lord, strong and mighty,
  the Lord, mighty in battle!
Lift up your heads, O gates!
  and be lifted up, O ancient doors!
  that the King of glory may come in.
Who is this King of glory?
  The Lord of hosts,
  he is the King of glory!

—Psalm 24

HOLY IS THE EARTH

"But I say to you, Do not swear at all, either by heaven, for it is the throne of God, or by the earth, for it is his footstool, or by Jerusalem, for it is the city of the great King. And do not swear by your head, for you cannot make one hair white or black."

—Matthew 5:34–36

Jesus' contemporaries knew that God's name is holy, and they chose to use other words for their oaths. They also knew that the earth is holy: "The earth is the Lord's, and the fulness thereof . . . ." But this they forgot.

This forgetfulness is even deeper and more common in our day, especially among those who hold God's name to be holy. For whenever we deny that *anything* is holy, or divide up the world into sacred and profane spheres, we conclude that there is an area, greater or smaller, in which there is no God.

The result appears to be a contradiction — on the one hand, contempt for this godless world, and on the other, a kind of religious submission to the powers of this world.

Contempt: things, beings, created man himself — all are looked upon as a kind of raw material. Man uses this material in whatever way he chooses, as bread or as poison, to build homes or to destroy homes, to sustain life or to annihilate it. It seems as though the raw material, even the human element, willingly permits itself to be used. One of the banal facts of life is that man's hair can be made to be either dark or light, according to whim. What is worse is that there are also methods for making one's soul dark or light. Under such circumstances it is easy to exploit the human body for purposes which would never be acceptable to man as a free being. Take, for example, dangerous or poorly paid work — not to mention certain forms of military service. If protest is in order, it seems so much less necessary with regard to so-called dead matter and the life which grows upon it. How strange and irrational is the Old Testament's regard for beasts of burden, who were due their day of rest, quite like men, and who sometimes received power to protest. I am thinking of the odd legend of Balaam's ass. "He struck the ass with his staff," we read. "Then the Lord opened the mouth of the ass, and she said to Balaam, 'What have I done to you, that you have struck me these three times?' " Stranger still is the idea that man can profane nature by criminal action. This is implied in God's word to Cain: "The voice of your brother's blood is crying to me from the ground. And now you are cursed from the ground, which has opened its mouth to receive your brother's blood from your hand."

But nature finally strikes back. As early as the third chapter of the Bible we read of the thorns and thistles which the earth bears and with which man must struggle. We can ask why the theft of the forbidden fruit should have such results. Or why, a couple of chapters later, the evil on earth should be punished with a flood. Or why David's adultery should result in a plague that afflicted not him but the people. But sometimes a connection between crime and punishment is perceivable. Many of the biblical judgments have, as a matter of fact, been brought about by man himself. The denominator common to fratricide and the spoliation of nature is a mentality. When man looks upon his environment as so much raw material, he is blind. All of a sudden he is confronted by such phenomena as soil ruination or the pollution of air and water, or by such fruits of soul destruction as bacteriological warfare. But such sudden catastrophes have as a rule required lengthy preparations. Man undermines his own existence gradually, beginning in his own heart, with the undermining of reverence for life.

But when such things happen, religious mentalities are usually busy being religious. What does the spiritual have to do with the secular? Why should man call upon God's name in defense of matter? What if the pale blue fields are strewn with nuclear fallout from our experiments? What if the earth becomes a desert? What if our cities, like cancerous growths, virtually consume the land around them? Theological discussions are disturbed only sporadically by such questions. As though they belonged to another world.

But alongside of this contempt appears another phenomenon, which the Sermon on the Mount describes thus: Man forgets that the earth is God's; yet he swears by it. This is because the soul really cannot be secularized; man is incurably religious. If there is no God in the world, the world becomes a god. If politics is divorced from religion, politics becomes a religion. It is the same with culture, careers, opinions.

Even many who believe that they believe in God can speak about the state of the market, the forming of opinion, structures of power, etc. in a tone of voice that denotes fear and submission. How should they dare to oppose progress?

In the face of this contempt, this superstitious servility, Christ teaches us that the earth is the Lord's — and that Jerusalem is "the city of the great King." The psalm just quoted utilizes both of these motifs. It asks, "Who shall ascend the hill of the Lord?/And who shall stand in his holy place?" And it replies, "He who has clean hands and a pure heart." The psalm ends by opening the gates for "the great King." "Lift up your heads, O gates!/and be lifted up, O ancient doors!/that the King of glory may come in."

When Jesus came to Jerusalem he cried over the city, not because its people were to kill him, but because it was going blindly to its destruction. A weeping king, powerless in the face of what was to come — what a contrast to our usual notion about such expressions as "the great," "glorious entrance," and similar rubrics.

But the streets have never been able to forget his footsteps, and an echo from the governor's palace rings down through the centuries: "So you are a king?" Jerusalem was not just so much raw material to be used for his own glory; its inhabitants were not there just to be organized, or to be used in spreading an idea. A sparrow fallen to the ground was not excluded from his prayer to the Father in heaven, even though he knew that two sparrows could be bought for a pittance.

He had innocent hands and a pure heart.

Thus it was that he loved God's world, heaven and earth, the city that surrounded him in its plenitude of power, and the individual who could not make one hair either white or black. Because of this, he could stand in the presence of power and authority without fear, without making obsequious requests for favor, without trying to persuade the opinion-makers. "So you are a king?"

Whence did this sovereign come? He is God's covenant with the world — with Jerusalem's temple and the sparrow on the ground, with the fire of heaven and the rain which gives new birth to the lilies. And with us all. In him profanity has been broken, and the earth is holy. In his name the basic elements have become signs that unite us with God. So it is that we are born again for eternal life through water and the Spirit. So it is that we break bread and discover an everlasting mercy in the fruit of the earth. So it is that we can live again in God's creation.

"Do not swear at all." Neither Creator nor creation exists to maintain our prestige. In the city of the great King, an entirely new alliance has been founded, and a security of an entirely different kind has been established. Grace streams down from heaven, for God permits it to rain on both the just and the unjust. Mercy grows out of the earth, which produces wheat from the time of creation to the night when the Lord is betrayed. No longer are things merely so much raw material. Everything is mystery, revelation, forgiveness of sin in the name of Jesus Christ. Blessed is he.

The Repressed Heaven

> Jacob left Beer-sheba, and went toward Haran. And
> he came to a certain place, and stayed there that
> night, because the sun had set. Taking one of
> the stones of the place, he put it under his head
> and lay down in that place to sleep. And he
> dreamed that there was a ladder set up on the
> earth, and the top of it reached to heaven; and
> behold, the angels of God were ascending and
> descending on it! And behold, the Lord stood
> above it and said, "I am the Lord, the God of
> Abraham your father and the God of Isaac; the
> land on which you lie I will give to you and to
> your descendants; and your descendants shall be
> like the dust of the earth, and you shall spread
> abroad to the west and to the east and to the north
> and to the south; and by you and your descendants
> shall all the families of the earth bless themselves.
> Behold, I am with you and will keep you where-
> ever you go, and will bring you back to this land;
> for I will not leave you until I have done that of
> which I have spoken to you." Then Jacob awoke
> from his sleep and said, "Surely the Lord is in
> this place; and I did not know it." And he was
> afraid, and said, "How awesome is this place! This
> is none other than the house of God, and this is
> the gate of heaven."
>
> —Genesis 28:10–17

Sometimes the angels in the Bible seem to be visible to the
eyes of man. They come out of space to make Christmas

night tremble with their songs of praise, and on St. Michael's day a tremendous thundercloud, in which the powers of dark and light are fighting each other, envelops us. But on some occasions they come from another kind of space — our dreams. So it is in this text.

Psychologists assert that we dream in order to keep from waking up. If the memories, the unrest, the expectations that occupy our minds during the night should confront us just as they do while we are awake, then we would suddenly wake up, and would probably be unable to fall asleep again. This is especially true of those things we would rather not think about, the things we very skillfully suppress during the day. When we go to sleep we can no longer do this; that which we suppressed during the day then confronts us — but in disguise. Anyone who would like to know his own secret thoughts ought to learn to unmask his dreams. What would Jacob have learned if he had done this?

One thing Jacob did understand as soon as he woke up. He had slept, without knowing it, in a holy place. This is what the angels say wherever they appear — on a river bank or among rocks, in the confusion of battle or in the quiet of the desert: "This must be a holy place; God most certainly dwells here."

To Jacob only certain places were holy, but from Jesus we learn that all places are holy. God does not dwell only in churches, and man does not live in God's presence only when he prays. No steps are needed between the heavenly world and us. The kingdom of heaven is at hand.

Jacob had a special reason for failing to note the kind of place he was in. And I am not only thinking of the fact that it was dark when he, weary as he was, sought a stone to serve as a pillow, nor am I thinking of the fact that he had never been in this area before. Jacob was fleeing his brother, whom he had deceived. He was fleeing an avenger. But he was also running away from guilt. Perhaps he had tried to convince himself that if he could only escape the revenge with which he was threatened he would also escape the guilt. A well-known critic of Christianity has written a book entitled *The Condition of Solace,* in which he asks how an adult can find a substitute for the advantage a child has in being able to go to his parents to receive forgiveness. He describes his solution to the problem thus: "Forgive me the wrong I have done as soon as I see that others have forgotten it."

He who feels that he is in a holy place cannot reason thus. That is probably why Jacob could not bring himself to recognize where he was. When he awoke he could say, as a poet said many years later: "If I say, 'Let only darkness cover me,/and the light about me be night,'/even the darkness is not dark to thee,/the night is bright as the day;/for darkness is as light with thee." This insight, which he had concealed from himself while he was awake, appeared with blinding clarity when he fell asleep.

But this dream of angels said something not only about the place where Jacob had slept, but also about a reality that Jacob took with him wherever he went. The gate to heaven could be found everywhere, for Jacob took with him everywhere this inner space in which angels appeared. He could flee his home but not his own heart, and so he could not flee God either.

And neither could he escape his guilt — for the same reason. It is significant that when God spoke to him in the dream it was not as Esau's God, but as the God of Abraham and Isaac. In this way a deeper layer of guilt was exposed in the dream. For the conflict that Jacob fled involved sibling rivalry only superficially. More properly, this was a parental conflict. Jacob was his mother's son. It was at her instigation that he pretended to be his brother in the presence of the blind old father. And it was the mother who sent him away to Haran, where her family dwelt. But a voice within said to Jacob, "I am your father's God . . . ."

There are schools of psychology which hold that all of us bear guilt feelings of this very kind. When one hears so much defiance of authority from those who would gladly be authorities themselves, one must wonder if many of our contemporaries do not harbor unresolved conflicts arising from their first experience with authority. Unbelief sometimes results from this same matrix. Men do not believe in God because he says, "I am your father's God . . . ."

One might be able to believe that the God of our dreams wants to humiliate the renegade and send him back home, approximately in the way authorities these days treat minors who run away from home. But God is not a policeman, even though many believe that he is. It is true that heaven is filled with light. One cannot find heaven without also discovering the truths that one seeks to flee, as well as the truths that have been hidden in the depths where dreams are born. It is also true that such a revelation has a quality of inevitability about it: How can you believe that you can flee God? Or escape guilt?

But God wanted to talk to Jacob about a blessing. Was it the blessing Jacob had stolen from his brother? The blessing of a blind man, conferred by mistake? We all have a bad conscience for the blessings we have not merited; one can even be so fearful of these that he dare not rejoice. It is as though all joy were stolen joy — for which we must pay a price. The dread of meeting God, which many feel, is similar to the dread a penniless man experiences in his anticipation of the moment when a bill is scheduled to arrive.

But it is obvious that God's blessing is not something that one can appropriate as he can money. Properly speaking, it was not Jacob who had the blessing; the blessing possessed Jacob. God said: "I am with you . . . ." This dreadful thought was then altered. He did not say, "I am with you and will punish you," but "I am with you and will keep you . . . ."

That heaven is near at hand in this way is not something that man dreams about by himself. One can dream of that terrible eye which is turned toward us day and night. One can dream of guilt and damnation — for the angels we have with us are the angels of judgment. But the blessing which no one merits, which is given without cost to whoever happens to be there — this does not come from within our hearts. Neither was this woven out of Jacob's dreams. He had brought this along from home. Originally, it had been given to his grandfather Abraham: "By your descendants shall all the nations of the earth bless themselves." This tradition had been passed on from father to son.

This tradition lives among us. We believe that this blessing referred to Jesus; in his name generation after generation has been blessed. And now the God of baptism says to us through this text: Do not be afraid of heaven; step forth in the light with your guilt, with everything. Light itself is a blessing, and Jesus Christ is its name. It is hard to believe this about God — that he pursues the fugitive in order to bless him — but it is precisely for this that we have the gospel: "I am with you . . . ."

Jacob traveled farther through the desert. He would eventually become a man in his own right, though it would take some time. One does not grow up simply as a result of leaving home. One does not become independent simply by running away from strong men. One's lack of maturity goes with him. But to live in the presence of God . . . . To experience a blessing in such a way that one dares to identify with himself — his childhood, his youth, his now — and to permit heaven to cast its light upon the deep-down guilt . . . . That is to be someone. As when Jacob returned to the land where God had first revealed himself to him. Then it was, at last, that he was ready to assume the name he was to have before God: "No longer shall your name be called Jacob, but Israel shall be your name."

Each one of us is also called to be someone before God. Be still in the presence of the gospel — that blessing through which the earth reveals its holiness. To flee the presence of heaven on earth is not merely to attempt to flee God. It is to attempt to run away from ourselves — from our deepest identity. Linger in the ribbon of light where the angels sing their songs of praise, and rediscover your name in the presence of God.

The King Without a Country

> And this is the testimony of John, when the
> Jews sent priests and Levites from Jerusalem to
> ask him, "Who are you?" He confessed, he did
> not deny, but confessed, "I am not the Christ."
> And they asked him, "What then? Are you Elijah?"
> He said, "I am not." "Are you the prophet?" And
> he answered, "No." They said to him then, "Who
> are you? Let us have an answer for those who sent
> us. What do you say about yourself?" He said,
> "I am the voice of one crying in the wilderness,
> 'Make straight the way of the Lord,' as the prophet
> Isaiah said."
> Now they had been sent from the Pharisees.
> They asked him, "Then why are you baptizing,
> if you are neither the Christ, nor Elijah, nor the
> prophet?" John answered them, "I baptize with
> water; but among you stands one whom you do
> not know, even he who comes after me, the thong
> of whose sandal I am not worthy to untie." This
> took place in Bethany beyond the Jordan, where
> John was baptizing.
>
> —John 1:19–28

"The Jews sent priests and Levites to him," we read. Later
on we discover that it was the Pharisees who stood behind
this deputation. We can be sure that none but the leading
Pharisees could use priests and Levites as messengers. It was
very fitting that the priests should make the inquiries, since
John himself came from a priest's family. Thus it was that

representatives of the nation's two principal classes, the priests and the Pharisees, confronted John and requested a straight answer. It was an important moment.

To us the questions seem to be what men call "spiritual" or "religious," and without significance when seen in the light of social and political realities. The fact is, however, that the air trembled with tension because of these questions, and John's answers had implications beyond measure for the entire nation.

Messiah — the royal title from the time of David and Solomon — was an office fraught with peril. The one who was then king of Israel was dependent upon the protection of Rome — a living contradiction of what the people meant by *Messiah*. Popular leaders who referred to themselves as *Messiah,* "the anointed one," were espousing insurrection and wars of liberation. And inasmuch as John had so much influence at that time, people thought, "Who knows?" It was of the utmost importance for the leading politicians to know his plans.

"Are you *Elijah?*" The prophet Malachi had promised the people that a new Elijah would appear before "the day of the Lord." If John did not want to grasp for the crown, as a beginning, perhaps he did desire to redeem the hope that fire would one day fall from heaven and destroy the heathen? A wave of national and religious enthusiasm — and then the Messiah, borne on its crest and powerful in its combined strength.

"Are you *the prophet?*" Moses had promised that. A prophet would rise up who was like him. "Him you shall heed" — so ran the promise. And had not the people listened to John? He might not wish to be called king, dangerous as that was, but might he nevertheless desire to give Israel a new Passover, and the oppressor a new experience of the Red Sea?

John had but one answer, and that was "No." But the

delegation would not be put off. Conscious of their importance, they pressed on: "Who are you then?" The answer came. "A voice," said John, "of one crying."

How strange it is that no one reacted to this answer. It was as though it had never been given. The Evangelist goes on to tell us who had sent the delegation, but says nothing about their response. John's statement was so important to the Evangelist that he had to be sure to tell us who it was ultimately to be meant for. This brief notice looks like a memorandum on a piece of registered mail: This is the address, and here is the name of the addressee. He will take the next step.

But the next step was not to be taken for some time. Now, the men from Jerusalem wanted to know who had authorized John to baptize. He had denied the titles of honor, he had refused to ascend the pedestal of fame, he spoke as though he did not understand the significance of the occasion. How did this harmonize with the baptism which drew crowds of people to the sacred, historic river, offering them cleansing, preparation, and consecration?

John pointed away from himself. If he was something more than a voice, then he was a slave, an oriental house slave who met his lord when he came home, loosened his shoes, and bathed his feet. John did not even feel worthy to do this. "Among you stands one whom you do not know." The servant hinted here at a sacred presence, and if the servant was so insignificant, what must his lord be like!

The disappointment the listeners felt can be read between the lines. The spark which should have set the situation on fire did not materialize. Those who sent out this clerical committee waited in vain for a definite answer. John's name continued to be an unknown factor in the political equation. The Baptist had said nothing. Or had he? "One whom you do not know." It was said of the Messiah that "when he comes, no one will know where he came from." The one who was awaited with apprehension was already there. Anonymous. This must have been unnerving.

And we say: They obviously did not want to listen when John said what he did about the voice; they knew all too well how this quotation from Isaiah continued: "Prepare the way of the Lord . . . ./Every valley shall be lifted up,/and every mountain and hill be made low." They were not interested in more sermons on repentance. As a result, they could not understand what John said about the one who stood in their midst. They didn't know him then, nor did they come to know him later on.

But we? Do we know him? Are our questions to the voice in the wilderness so unlike those put by the priests?

Not all who have been asked if they were the Messiah have answered as John did. "The world will prosper according to the desires of mankind's progressive powers, and the future will bring peace, freedom and well-being to all men." These are the concluding words in a book commonly distributed at civil confirmation ceremonies in a certain European country. Directly beneath are the pictures of four messianic figures, the fourth of whom was still alive when this book was published. A number of Christians have been imprisoned for opposing this book. Why this opposition? What has Christ to do with politics?

In other parts of the world men depend upon revival to provide the ultimate defense against this universal plan of redemption. Or they trust in technical progress. Fire from the sky shall defend freedom. Scientific triumphs shall make it possible to conquer the Red Sea.

These are old questions, questions about rulers, about prophets of fire, about heroes of freedom. The messianic questions. They have whipped up expectations to religious dimensions; eternity and the kingdom of heaven loom before those who labor and are heavy laden. And when these expectations fail to materialize they collapse, and collapsed expectations are identical with anguish. Men have chosen to provide their rulers and cultures and political systems with saving virtues and divine powers, and only when it is too late do they ask these messiahs who they are, what they have to say for themselves, and by what right they preach.

And what does the church say? All too often she has given herself the most distinguished of names. Neither the Messiah's crown nor the prophet's mantle has been lacking in these designations.

Or else she has humbled herself before the powers that be — becoming their house slave, submissively awaiting their arrival, lending them her voice, proclaiming their victories and setting their misdeeds aside. Fawning upon them when asked for information, or crying out in self-defense and self-glorification in order to win their favor.

"Prepare the way" — that is what the church is called to proclaim. She should preach repentance so that the practical politicians may be disappointed. Disappointed — not because the church has spoken indistinctly or ignored burning realities, but because she has grated and irritated by speaking out for the right ways in precisely those areas where such talk was uncomfortable.

But this is not the heart of our text. The most important thing is not the way, but the one who travels on it: "one whom you do not know." The man in the middle, the answer to questions ancient and modern, the fulfillment of prophecies before John and after the apostles. We have asked what he and his messengers have to do with that book in which the way to eternal peace is mapped out. Answer: He is the alternative. Not a romantic decoration or a faded, pious dream. But the one who deserves the veneration we give to politics, technology, culture, and to all of their messiahs, the one who alone can wear the crown of our expectations, our longing for God. And this he did in the midst of fragile reality, victimized by the plan which proved to be the final answer to John's testimony. The plan which was to put him to death.

"One whom you do not know." Do we know him? The king without a country. The prophet who didn't even know who had struck him. The popular leader who traveled alone. Love's alternative. The God who untied the shoes of a tired envoy and dried his servant's feet. The God who waits like a house slave for the time when the poor come home and sinners pound on the door.

"One whom you do not know." But tell that to the regents and the parliaments, to culture prophets and folk heroes: *"This* is the Lord; put the world in order for his coming — not only the church, but the world, that which you call reality." And the world will recognize him, put John in jail, and unleash its hate to charge like a roaring lion on the roads by which Christ draws near.

"Among you." The church says that he is here. It isn't John who speaks in the gospel, but the one who came after him. The one who became bread for the hungry. If this is true — just think! Just think if that dangerous answer, which can cause a man to be arrested and despised, were proclaimed loud and clear in the church! Just think if he, who is worthy of our suffering because he is the suffering Messiah, were actually to give the weary and the anxious the only alternative to what the world provides — and do that here and now.

We have referred to the delegation's response to John's declaration, whose meaning did not become clear until later on. In many instances, as here in our text, there is hardly a response at all. There is a certain satisfaction, or a certain feeling of discomfort, but no words, no deeds. As though the preacher hadn't said a thing.

Sometimes preachers *don't* say anything. If John had said that Jesus was to be found in religious mysteries far from the exercise of power — and therefore beyond all social, political, and cultural problems — the deputation would have been surprised, presumably, but appeased. And that art of preaching has some ancient traditions: to give the impression, for example, that Christ came to serve only in the spiritual and religious sense, not in flesh and blood, not in time and space. But this is really quite different: "among you." When this assertion was finally verified by the fact that Christ intruded upon the very center of Jewish existence, then the world found him dangerous, while sinners found him wonderful. Both of these are characteristic of the true gospel; they go together. If the church is not dangerous to the world, then the world does not endanger the church, but those who are preyed upon by the powers of society and of their own hearts are imperiled and betrayed. Mercy and forgiveness are the fruit of Christ's victory over the powers, and if we lose sight of that victory, then nothing of the miracle of redemption will remain for the care of souls and the care of society, except a bit of pious and harmless amiability.

But even a gospel in which the presence of Christ is perceptible can be totally ignored by many for a long time (save as a kind of Advent mood, or some other form of decoration). If the committee had come without preconceived formulas concerning salvation and the Messiah, they would not have had to return home unhappy, their mission a failure. The fact of the matter is that the Messiah can appear before the eyes of all without being noticed by everyone. There is judgment in this fact, mysteriously inserted into the essence of the gospel. One of the distinguishing characteristics of the Messiah is that he can go unrecognized. He is such that we prefer to limit our witness concerning his presence — unless our thirst after God breaks through our defense, those reservations and conventions which dictate what he can be and how he can act. "And this is the judgment," writes John the Evangelist, "that the light has come into the world, and men loved darkness rather than light, because their deeds were evil." Evil deeds must be hidden — even when this merely involves the protection of privilege, prosperity, and the status quo in the face of threats from others who are situated differently.

But of many who, after hearing the gospel, return home to an unruffled existence and an impotent piety it can be said, as of the priests and Levites sent out by the Pharisees: "They could have seen God."

I

2. And the Last

Fortune Telling

> *Being asked by the Pharisees when the kingdom
> of God was coming, he answered them, "The
> kingdom of God is not coming with signs to be
> observed; nor will they say, 'Lo, here it is!' or
> 'There!' for behold, the kingdom of God is in the
> midst of you."*
>
> *And he said to the disciples, "The days are
> coming when you will desire to see one of the
> days of the Son of man, and you will not see it.
> And they will say to you, 'Lo, there!' or 'Lo, here!'
> Do not go, do not follow them. For as the light-
> ning flashes and lights up the sky from one side to
> the other, so will the Son of man be in his day. But
> first he must suffer many things and be rejected by
> this generation. As it was in the days of Noah, so
> will it be in the days of the Son of man. They ate,
> they drank, they married, they were given in mar-
> riage, until the day when Noah entered the ark,
> and the flood came and destroyed them all. Like-
> wise as it was in the days of Lot—they ate, they
> drank, they bought, they sold, they planted, they
> built, but on the day when Lot went out from
> Sodom fire and brimstone rained from heaven and
> destroyed them all—so will it be on the day when
> the Son of man is revealed."*
>
> —Luke 17:20–30

When the Pharisees asked about the coming of the kingdom
of God, and when Jesus spoke of the coming of the Son of
man, the discussion centered upon a passage from Daniel:
"I saw in the night visions,/and behold, with the clouds of

heaven/there came one like a son of man . . . . /And to him was given dominion/and glory and kingdom,/that all peoples, nations, and languages/should serve him;/his dominion is an everlasting dominion,/which shall not pass away, /and his kingdom one/that shall not be destroyed." In Jesus' time, as in many other times, there were theologians who felt that they could determine when this would occur. These reckonings have frequently assumed that the Son of man would dwell on earth for a while prior to the coming of the kingdom, and that he would then live incognito, known only to a few, until the day of judgment had come.

Jesus drew a line through this biblical mathematics, these chronicles of years and weeks, these lists of kings and imperial epochs. And he gave no support to those popular enthusiasts who asserted, now here and now there, that they had seen heaven on earth. Such calculations are supported by neither time nor place. All of a sudden the day comes — as the flood over Noah's generation, as the fire over Sodom. And this is certainly not first proclaimed in certain local announcements; it is, rather, like a flash of lightning which reaches from the east to the west. This is an event of cosmic dignity.

We need to have but one portent: "But first he [the Son of man] must suffer many things and be rejected by this generation." Jesus combined the prophecy of the Son of man, who was to come on the clouds, with Isaiah's picture of the suffering servant: "He was despised and rejected by men;/ a man of sorrows, and acquainted with grief."

This was a new and upsetting proclamation — then. But we know, of course, that what was to happen "first" took place rather soon, if the Evangelist is right — and very long ago, as seen from our point of view. These events say nothing to us about the future, much less about the end of time.

Is this then anything to preach today, this claim that a certain historical person, known as Jesus of Nazareth, shall one day come again as a kind of a sign in the heavens? Is it credible that this Galilean is coming to put an end to the history of the world, and to do it in this unusual manner? Were not all of these ideas concocted in a small country where man's conceptual powers never took in more than a little time and a little space? How irrational these ideas seem today, two thousand years later, when we live under the heavens of modern astronomy.

There are "spaces" which cannot be gauged by a telescope. There are measures of time other than years and centuries. As when Jesus said, "But first the Son of man must suffer . . . ." What system of measurements applies to suffering? Suffering follows time like a ray of darkness; no one saw its beginning, no one has seen its end. And if one selects a point on this ray, the suffering of a single individual during one specific hour, not only is that point a particular part of all of the suffering in the world but it also has its own dimension, a hole bored down into existence itself — and who can know its depth? If this person says, "I can endure it, I can endure even more" — how long is "endurance," and how can this be classified in order to serve as a gauge or a measure?

The only way to take the measure of suffering is to experience it. We are usually forced to this, but some experience it without being forced to do so. The ones who love. They also realize that it is far to the depths of suffering, farther than their love can reach. *Their* love.

And when Jesus said that "the Son of man must suffer," how far did that "must" reach? This is not merely a question of fulfilling Old Testament prophecy. There is more than visions and inspiration from above behind the words Isaiah spoke concerning the suffering servant. Suffering itself is there. A nation's suffering. Other texts reflect this same reality, all the way from Genesis 4, where the blood of Abel cries from the ground, to the words in Revelation about the final tribulation, the last wave of anguish and suffering — and the martyrs' question: "Lord, how long?" This torment which surrounds mankind with its questions about God, its doubts about God, its cries after God — this is the "must" of Jesus Christ. If the Son of man is God of God, light of light, and if God is love — then he must suffer, suffer here among us, with us, then he must take the measure of the width and depth of this sea, our anguish.

And when he took upon himself this "must," then we saw that reality on Calvary bore his features. As a shadow, or a remarkable negative. Suffering is itself a sign telling us that we are near the border — a prophetic question concerning someone who opened this sealed book. One day the answer was here, crucified in our history. And there is nothing in the book which is not contained in those years, those days, those hours when "the Son of man must suffer."

Therefore, says the gospel, this Galilean shall put an end to history, because he has suffered through it in love. The sign of suffering is no longer anonymous. It lifts the Son of man above time. Now we know who it is that is coming. The one on the cross.

This sign says the same thing today as two thousand years ago. The space surrounding the cross has not been altered by our explorations into space. *This* is the cosmos of suffering.

There are two ways of failing to notice this sign.

The one is to believe that one either has the formula or is on the way to finding it. I refer to the formula for heaven and earth. The formula for God. Those who know this stand there with their figures and calculations and discuss the kingdom of God. They invite Jesus to come along and compute. They neither see nor understand that the Son of man, about whom they ask questions, stands right before them, and that God's kingdom is thus in the midst of them.

This blindness remains the same from age to age. It professes to know what God ought actually to be like, and how he really acts. Or else it professes to know that God cannot actually exist, since man seems unable to make the reality and the act consistent. In both instances, men shut their eyes to the sign that has been carved into our humanity, the Christ-sign, and at the same time they join forces with those who raised this sign on Golgotha. For this also — this very rejection — is one of the signals indicating that time is a borderland. This also proclaims which kingdom, and whose kingdom, will meet us on the other side: the Son of man must first "be re-jected by this generation."

The other way to ignore this sign is described in our text by examples drawn from the time of Noah and the time of Lot. Here it is not a question of so controlling life that it can serve as an arithmetical example. It is a question of avoiding all real thought about life. To eat and drink, carry on one's business, read the social pages in the daily paper. To adjust oneself to what "they" say and think and do. To be sure that nothing can be important unless everyone says so, that noth-ing has real weight and significance unless "they say so." This is like living in a newspaper column, or on a TV tube. Ulti-mately one can't even see the sun or the stars if they have not been reviewed. But on the day Noah went into the ark he was given no publicity; there were too many other things going on. And we are told that on the day when Lot left Sodom he tried to convince his sons-in-law to join him; they thought he was joking. So Noah was rejected, and Lot too. So is the Son of man rejected, to the end of time. Once again the sign is raised over those who do not have faith in it, the sign that bears the touch of him who suffered and was rejected.

Thus it is that in Advent we are called upon to challenge the "self-evident" conclusions that are built upon shortsighted calculations, our own and others'. Thoughtlessness itself is something for us to think about; the very security we find in the infallibility of others' opinions is a warning signal for us. And if we take ourselves beyond the region of false security and seek for truth and reality — what will we find?

That suffering cries out. That someone is suffering and thus crucified, someone who loves. In addition, this: When it seems that nothing but darkness remains, then his presence causes the darkness to shine. So in the end it is not lightning that enables us to understand how his face will at one time be seen by all men who dwell on earth. Not lightning or the clouds of heaven, not intercontinental television or new concepts concerning time and space. But the fact that he is in our midst. The fact that around the world those who commune at the altar meet him and say, "We have seen his glory." The gospel fills the cosmos of suffering with his nearness. As Paul says: "neither . . . things present, nor things to come, nor powers, nor height, nor depth . . . will be able to separate us from the love of God in Christ Jesus our Lord."

We know that God's kingdom is coming, because it is already here. An everlasting mercy is here. Jesus Christ is here.

The Movement of Time

> *"Again, the kingdom of heaven is like a net which was thrown into the sea and gathered fish of every kind; when it was full, men drew it ashore and sat down and sorted the good into vessels but threw away the bad. So it will be at the close of the age. The angels will come out and separate the evil from the righteous, and throw them into the furnace of fire; there men will weep and gnash their teeth."*
>
> —Matthew 13:47–50

Anyone who has ever helped to draw in a seine will reexperience a feeling of impatience as he reads this parable. Drawing a seine is a tedious job, you see, and as the seine comes closer to shore, tension grows. It is not until the sack is finally drawn up to land that the fishermen can tell what they have caught. Then the sorting can begin.

It is this idea of not knowing until the last minute that, like a kind of double exposure, leads over to the second picture set forth in our text, that of the last day: "So it will be at the close of the age." The impatient waiting which cannot be disassociated from the drawing of the seine will also characterize the last judgment. This seems surprising inasmuch as judgment is, for most people, a thunderstorm in the distance, so dark and obscure that many wonder if there really is such a thing as judgment. What of the person who looks forward to this? Might this not reflect an attitude of prideful innocence, a brass-plated ignorance of the fact that all men are implicated in the guilt of this world?

In contrast, members of the early church could speak of judgment as a mercy and say, "May grace come, and this world pass away." The church of that era had had bloody experience with judgments not rendered by God – judgments like the one that crucified Jesus. It was the church that was then under sentence. Because of this, Christian men had reason to ask if there was righteousness in the world, righteousness and mercy. The answer to that is this: The time will come when all injustice will be tested. Isn't that something to look forward to, even today? I am not thinking only of those who have been imprisoned because of their faith, men like Dietrich Bonhoeffer and Cardinal Mindszenty, nor only of the anti-Christian propaganda heard in certain lands. The church itself has often been guilty of making unrighteous judgments. I am thinking above all of the judgments which are pronounced among us without either investigation or trial. There are many examples of this, both in the press and in our daily conversation. Many who indignantly reject the idea of a Last Judgment – could a God of love judge anyone? – sit in judgment upon their neighbors every day, calling them unfriendly, boring, beyond help. And such judgments are pronounced without the slightest show of mercy. There is also a kind of guilt sadism that goes about with delicate intimations and says, "It was your fault." This conduct reflects a sick conscience as yet unrecognized by the one who possesses it. The fact is that the culprit himself is relieved to see the guilt burden of others increase, especially if he is trying to escape an awareness of his own guilt.

But the day will come when all this shall end, when oppressed justice shall arise and render speechless the innumerable opinion-makers who through the centuries have pronounced what men call the judgments of history. This is really something to look forward to. The evaluations which biased people make of, say, the lynching of a Negro in the United States or a banal scandal in Sweden, summarily described in an advertising slogan: "For a limited time only."

Both the judges and the condemned may find it hard to believe in final judgment. Erroneous headlines are sometimes corrected, but in the back pages of the paper; such are the proportions between truth and untruth in this world. But we hear no motion for a new trial; the last word is determined by public relations and money.

But there are signs that the truth is on the way. The weightiest of these is the light that proceeds from the one who told us the parable of the net. This light is such that it does not permit itself to be used to judge others. The way it operates is described in the report of another fishing expedition, which ended when Peter said to the one who had helped him, "Depart from me, for I am a sinful man." Anyone at all can choose to ignore what people say about him — praise or blame — and turn to Christ, as he meets us in the texts, with a request which the psalmist formulates thus: "Search me." Otherwise we all stand on guard against every kind of judgment, constantly prepared to defend ourselves before others and, above all, before ourselves. If the judgment of Christ should be pronounced in the same way as others, we would still defend ourselves: "It wasn't I; on the contrary, haven't I been a friend to my neighbor, to all? And what can you really expect of me — of one who has known so little joy in this life?" But now our defense is silenced, simply because the judgment of Christ speaks from within our own condition. It comes from one who was condemned and forsaken, from one who in this situation loved us all.

Exposed, and yet loved: after such an experience, one realizes that he stands under a judgment that is not man's. And then it is easier to see the other signs that testify in secret to the fact that the truth is near. The people who sort out fish on a beach — or perhaps sand in a gravel pit, or light bulbs in a factory — are shown in this light to be unknowing witnesses. This judgment is not the whim of someone who intrudes from outside, saying, "That is enough, now." This is a power from within, invisibly exerting its influence, a mysterious presence which makes itself known to those who have eyes to see. This is not an ecclesiastical specialty, but an activity in time — yes, time's own activity. The net which is slowly drawn ashore, filled, as the basic Greek text says, with "all kinds," provides the banal expression "time goes by" with unexpected meaning. Yes, times goes by, perhaps in the direction of world peace, or perhaps in the direction of a war which will poison earth, water, and air. But in all of this and beyond all of this, time is moving toward clarity, toward new heavens and a new earth in which — and this is the important thing — righteousness dwells.

The Friend Whom I Seek Above All

> *Be patient, therefore, brethren, until the coming of
> the Lord. Behold, the farmer waits for the precious
> fruit of the earth, being patient over it until it re-
> ceives the early and the late rain. You also be
> patient. Establish your hearts, for the coming of the
> Lord is at hand. Do not grumble, brethren, against
> one another, that you may not be judged; behold,
> the Judge is standing at the doors. As an example
> of suffering and patience, brethren, take the proph-
> ets who spoke in the name of the Lord.*
>
> —James 5:7–10

The author of these lines clearly believed that Christ's return and the Last Judgment could be expected at any time.
Some who today read what he wrote might therefore lose confidence in him — for we are accustomed to judge reliability by
exactness in statements concerning space and time. James's
calculations do not stand up, and we are therefore finished
with him and with the Second Coming and judgment and
all such.

Many people will find the fact that James presupposes a
longing for that which is called the Second Coming even
stranger than his calculations. The Second Coming implies,
of course, that many will not be finished with that for which
they really lived. Young lovers who have long awaited their
wedding day will never see it; the artist who threw his whole
being into his work will never complete it; the businessman
who recently expanded his interest will never realize his profit.
And that is not all. If this world ceases to exist, there will no

longer be any love, any art, or any enterprise. In that case, what will have been the use of all this? Shall the generations suddenly be cut off, shall culture and social progress end in an empty nothingness? Is this something to look forward to with great impatience?

These objections go together. For that which we are so unwilling to leave behind has been attained in part by the use of just such calculations as we found to be lacking in James — and many believe that as a result we have found the secret of life. We have so adjusted ourselves and our children to this point of view that heaven itself comes as an unpleasant surprise.

But James does not look upon time and the world as so much raw material to be used to make a fortune or to build an ideal state. He sees it rather as a field. Someone has sown that field, and now it rains. Thus it was that James's world waited for summer. Something germinated beneath the surface, and soon burst through. The entire matter is similar to a natural process. One can accommodate oneself to it, as a farmer does, but one cannot stop it; the sun and the rain cannot be stopped. We are talking here about forces and events that are not subject to human command. And this is why James miscalculated the date of the Second Coming; he was wrong because he was right with respect to the question itself, for this is a question which cannot be solved in the same way as a business calculation. We cannot know God's spring and God's fall in terms of our days and our weeks; we do not have his almanac.

James's time, his world, matured in its way, and then began to decay. After a number of severe crises it burst apart, and a new history resulted, for he who sends the rain and the sunshine chose to take a number of crops from his fields. The result was not the Second Coming but what we know as church history.

Our text testifies to the dangers implicit in this transition — for the church and for faith. For when the Second Coming disappeared as a daily expectation, the sorrows of time took its place, both for the individual and for the church. Calculations resulted, the long-range kind, and it became much more important to succeed, to gain influence, to guarantee the morrow. Persecutions and other catastrophes, which had previously been interpreted as the harbingers of heaven, came to be looked upon as portents of the church's demise. The heirs of the kingdom of heaven came to think of themselves as heirs of the estate. It wasn't easy to follow the example of the prophets and endure suffering when many suspected that the prophecies had missed the mark.

And when the church began to look to the future instead of to eternity, then, by degrees, it became important not only that the church should obtain influence, but that the right persons should obtain influence in the church. When the church was no longer the ferry across the river to another reality, then it became the church of the Fathers, involving the defense of tradition and the selection of the right Church Fathers. We have no right to underestimate these debates, for they have actually assisted in the preservation of the pure gospel. But that which James describes as grumbling has also been preserved in its pure state: "Do not grumble, brethren, against one another." Even then men recognized the limits beyond which it did not pay to reason together, beyond which men were silenced by the stubbornness of the opposition; and instead of talking to deaf ears, they shrugged their shoulders and grumbled. Biblical humor enables us to visualize two churchmen in the last phase of a debate, face to face, exchanging complaints in a grumblers' dialogue.

We ought not to forget this either, that the Second Coming does not simply represent the end of the old order and the beginning of a time of judgment. It has a face — the Lord's.

The young Christian can still find a living witness to the Lord's activities. I can imagine how a cross-examination might proceed:

"You saw Lazarus come out of the tomb?"

"Yes, I saw that; he found it hard to walk, because he tripped on the grave clothes."

"And you were sure he had been dead?"

"Of course. The odor remained in the grave for a long time."

"Do you believe that the Lord was sure of that too?"

"I saw him cry!"

Silence. The youth turns away. For he didn't ask about miracles! He wanted to hear someone say, "I saw him!"

And we! Have we not also made pilgrimages to Bethany, to Cana, to Nain, to Nazareth! We have read, with an inward ache, what the witnesses have written: "which we have seen with our eyes, which we have looked upon and touched with our hands." To have seen the Lord!

And when the skies of the Second Coming fade away, leaving us with an empty heaven, then it is that this perfect tense becomes all the more important. For this was, of course, the promise: that we should get to see the Son of man coming . . . .

But this is not the whole truth about church history.

For when that which began in Galilee (expected for centuries by the prophets) spread over the earth like a new sowing, then it was still true, as one could say about the world which first heard the gospel: it is sown; something is being prepared under the surface, while events and eras pass over it like skies and rain.

What then? The answer is Christ. Church history is *also* Christ, the hidden Christ. Our world is pregnant with this. For it bears the gospel; the gospel is a hidden but wonderful presence. This means that everything we refer to as progress and time and the course of the world shall enter upon its final travail when the time — God's time — is ripe. What was true of the world in which James lived is true of ours. The fact that our world is so much larger alters nothing — all the more so because it is written that the last crop will cover the entire earth.

Those who know that Christ is the secret of time also know that he is its fulfillment. When time ends and meets its judge, this will not be the work of a stranger. This calls to mind the time when Jesus halted the funeral cortege outside the city gates, for he would not see a mother cry ("Do not weep"). He then spoke those fearful words to the young man: "I say to you, arise" — and gave him to his mother. So it is that he will put an end to the course of the world. The world will recognize its anguish, its suffering, its longing. Love, songs, the cities we have built and the woods in which we have gotten lost — they are all empty arms reaching out for someone, filled with a mysterious unrest and a powerful desire to see the Lord. Because this is so, the end of the world will not be something cruel and meaningless; it will judge everything and give meaning to everything. It is he for whom everything reaches, as the mountain ash reaches for the light. It is the Lord!

And he who becomes sufficiently calm to sense the goal of his unrest, what will he do? It is possible that he will find more than the stubbornness of others to complain about. He will have a double errand to those who report that the Lord is not ashamed to call us brothers. In part to experience thus that the judge is near — the one who judges us when we are ashamed of those he loves. In part to experience judgment at the point where it deepens into grace — as in the Lord's Supper, where he is not ashamed to receive such curious brothers, where the judge is literally near, clearing his way toward sinners in a mercy that draws blood.

Such he was. And such shall come. Who shall come? A

young man, around thirty years old when we last saw him.
The reverend apostles called him master, and the publicans
and sinners thought of him as friend. At any rate, that is
what his enemies said.

Distress, misunderstanding, suffering, anguish — but someone stands there at the custom house, looking out toward the
road on the other side of the barrier.

"What are you looking for?"

"I am waiting for a friend."

"Friend? What do you have for friends, you miserable tax
collector?"

"Yes, I have a friend, and he is coming, he is coming."

"No friend will come to you."

"Yes, he has promised; it is certain. I am waiting for my
friend."

"Be patient, therefore, brethren. . . ." Where is this expectation observed? Just think if the attitude of suffering and the
complaining disappeared for a time from the church and from
the debate over Christianity! If the Second Coming amounted
to more than a bit of theology, with or without calculations!
(We are aware of course of the schools which represent such
an "eschatology," and we also know what we need to know
about the matter!) The remarkable thing, generally speaking, is that people also groan when they think about the
Second Coming that they connect with secularization or with
Hiroshima or with certain astronomical facts. But where is the
connection with the Lord?

The women in Israel met David, after he had crushed the
Philistines, "with song and dance, with shouts of joy, drums
and triangles."

And Bach, in his cantata *Wachet auf (Wake! Awake!)* in-
troduced a dance melody which floated like a breath of air in
the crown of an aspen tree. It is Zion's daughter who meets
her King. It is the entire company of slaves and sinners and

43

wretches who meet their Savior. It is avalanches and dangerous storms and foaming waves which throw themselves against the depth of love which has drawn them to itself. It is all the larks who rise out of the valleys until the morning sun makes their wings shine. It is a dragonfly, blue with ice-crystal wings, casting herself out over a forest lake, and the forest murmurs in her dance. It is a praying man who opens his eyes and sees God. His friend has come.

Recapitulation

I

Then I saw a great white throne and him who sat upon it; from his presence earth and sky fled away, and no place was found for them.
—Revelation 20:11

The gospel tells us that the fullness of time is a reality. This does not mean that we shall one day see how well things have been organized for our enjoyment and how nicely our lives fit into a pleasant and harmonious pattern. Meaning has been destroyed, history has been broken into small pieces, and the puzzle does not fit together. Nevertheless, in the midst of meaninglessness a dramatic hidden meaning is at work.

Joseph was rejected by his brothers and sold into slavery. When his brothers next saw him, as the second most powerful man in Egypt, he said: "You meant evil against me; but God meant it for good." A mysterious purpose was at work in all of their evil thoughts. And gradually a theme which recurs with increased power can be discerned in this holy history: the righteous may suffer as Job did, the chosen may be cast in a pit as Jeremiah was. And when, at last, the entire chosen people was deported to the East, the motif was repeated: those who seek for meaning may experience meaninglessness.

Finally that which happened to the chosen people was outlined in the contours of a person: "He was despised and rejected by men;/a man of sorrows, and acquainted with grief . . . ;/yet we esteemed him stricken,/smitten by God, and afflicted." That is a literary interpretation of the situation. To be a Jew was to experience most painfully what it is to be a man — and this was not the last time. But many centuries later in this vortex of the human race a face appeared. Not a figure of speech, as when the prophet referred to the nation as a suffering servant, but a man of flesh and blood. The gospels tell us how he, so to speak, recapitulated the history of his people: at the beginning of his public ministry we find a report of the forty days spent in the desert, and at the beginning of his life on earth we are told of a flight which ended the same way as when the nation returned home after forty years in the wilderness: "Out of Egypt have I called my son." At the very last he descended into the deepest meaninglessness and was put to death while the mob yelled. And when Christendom rehearses this drama on Good Friday, these ancient words from the subsoil of Jewish history are always heard: "Surely he has borne our griefs/and carried our sorrows." Thus it was that he submitted himself to our history. But those who would strike him in the face did not manage to do so until they had tied a blindfold around his eyes.

And just as the past converged in the events which then took place in Jerusalem, so also has the history of the future radiated from this point. Properly speaking, there have been no ages after Christ — even though many have failed to notice how this relates to them: "Lord, when did we see thee hungry . . . and did not minister to thee?" Like a mighty wave, the gospel has gone forth through history to make us conscious of the kind of life we live. We can see ourselves in the things which happened to him. But this is an insight which one cannot grasp in a day. In many respects, Jesus' words, "they know not what they do," continue to be valid — and the drama is by no means diminished by the fact that we are so often involved without being aware of it.

So when history, like a magnetic field, assumes this pattern as a result of what happened in Bethlehem and on Golgotha, it is not only man whom we learn to know — man who suffers, man who seeks for meaning and ends up with meaninglessness. The gospel says that it is the love of God which aches forth in Christ's humanity. Love from on high, tender sympathy from above, does not tell us much — and so we also read in the Scriptures that "no one has ever seen God." But the Evangelist immediately goes on to say that "the only-begotten Son has made God known." This is the gospel of meaning, whose influence is exerted from the depths. And all of a sudden this gospel burst forth in the form of a wandering Jewish rabbi who associated with the untouchables and who loved those who were not considered worthy of love. He was the friend of tax collectors and sinners. And when this love suffered it did not take the form of celestial poetry or quiet music above the clouds; it suffered in human categories. Thus it was that the interrupted theme was restored. So it is that there is meaning in our midst, not a philosophy of the universe, but a living face which suffered under Pontius Pilate and under thousands of unknown power-wielders who also did not know what they were doing.

But the time is coming, according to Revelation, when this hidden drama will no longer be hidden. The mystery will shatter like a communion wafer, and out of this will come clarity. We shall then confront our deeds and perceive that they belong to a larger context, that they are both good and evil; and the idea of their meaninglessness will thereby be dispelled. This is a gift, for it is a relief to recognize oneself as an evil man if one has come to believe that there is no good or evil and that it makes no difference how one lives. There is no greater hell than that. But human weakness is not the only thing that will be revealed when the curtain opens on this drama. We shall also find love from the depths, and its eyes will not be blindfolded. We shall find it beyond history, beyond the Eucharist which otherwise epitomizes to the very end of time our relationship to Christ. We shall find it even though it is not imbedded in matter, or in anything earthly or human as in Galilee and at the altar. We shall find it in nakedness. The fire which burned in history shall be fire only, the face shorn of its mysterious veil. This is a fearful thought: the truth — and we have no eyeshade; love — a love more violent, more patient, more proud, more humble than everything we on earth commonly call love, a love which waited for us through a myriad of years and centuries — now we shall find it, and it will no longer be silent, as when it suffered; it will speak. "From his presence earth and sky fled away . . . ."

Then will this day too be exposed to the light, and meaninglessness shall be no more. As a sunbeam enters a dark room and transforms the dust into a multitude of stars, so shall it be with our days, the quiet, gray, uneventful, the aching, hopeless, tearstained, the love-filled, hate-filled, sin-filled, prayer-filled, bloodred days — all shall be touched by the light which transforms; they shall be as fire. This very day is included, for it is included in the gospel of love which reaches up to us from below.

II

> Then I saw a new heaven and a new earth; for the first heaven and the first earth had passed away, and the sea was no more. And I saw the holy city, new Jerusalem, coming down out of heaven from God, prepared as a bride adorned for her husband.
> —Revelation 21:1–2

When the haze disperses at the end of time, when heaven and earth pass away, space will not stand empty and silent.

There will be a new heaven and a new earth. Something is going to happen. God will create, just as in the beginning — "and God said, 'Let there be light.'" The cosmos will emerge anew — heaven, earth, and the seas — a swarm of living creatures, a shimmering garden of Eden.

This will not simply be a repetition of what took place the first time. God is not a poet who repeats himself. This is what eye has not seen and what the heart of man cannot envision. Yet it will not be entirely unfamiliar. For, strictly speaking, it will begin when the old world bursts — not as a bomb but as a seed. The new spring will be the continuation of something.

"And I heard a voice from heaven like the sound of many waters and like the sound of loud thunder; the voice I heard was like the sound of harpers playing on their harps, and they sing a new song before the throne and before the four living creatures and before the elders." This new creation will be built up around a musical theme, "a new song," but those who sing will be the hundred and forty-four thousand with the name of the Lamb on their foreheads. "The Lamb" — here is a carryover from the history of Israel. It was Israel which was slaughtered like a sacrificial lamb because its people were called upon to seek for meaning in the midst of meaninglessness. "The Lamb" — this is he who stepped into this history with God's own passion and who loved us from the very depths of powerlessness, despair, and suffering. The theme of the new creation was first sounded in Nazareth when God Almighty tumbled from his throne of majesty to the depths of our humanity. The tone of this seeking, suffering, burning, passionate love shall fill the new cosmos. A small Jewish village was the womb in which this world was begotten.

But that is to say that the history which died has begun again. For our history is summarized in the one who suffered on Golgotha. Out of the depths of confusion and meaninglessness, out of the reeking grave, out of the dark recesses of human nature our history arises like a refined *Te Deum,* a song of love. "And I saw the holy city, new Jerusalem, coming down out of heaven from God, prepared as a bride adorned for her husband."

When the church confesses this gospel, it is speaking of the resurrection of the dead. The new world is not a dilution of humanity into a series of isolated souls. It is a continuation in a new creation of our human totality, both in body and soul. We are not merely thoughts and moods, you know; we are related to the grass and the reeds, to the beetles and the waxwings: "from the earth you have come." No one of us can exist apart from a milieu. Someone gave birth to us, and new life emerges as a result of our love. A song in hot blood when the entire cosmos is contained in one embrace. The work which we planned together on a night when we could not sleep. The comrades who helped us, the plans which took form under our hands. The prelude we loved, a painting by Marc Chagall, a poem by Pär Lagerkvist. All of this and a thousand other details which stand out against the totality of life like trees on a distant ridge — all of this goes to make up that which is you or I, and this together with its historical roots and all of its branches in the present will be born anew when the new heaven and the new earth appear. Eternal life is not a bouquet of cut flowers in a vase somewhere in a celestial drawing room. The gospel speaks of the whole man, his roots included. The entire human tangle is involved, not just certain bits and pieces. Everything that the Bible embraces, beginning with the fact that we were created out of dust, brothers to the baboon and sisters to the pomegranate, and including the fall of the last great world state — all of this will be called into life anew on the other side of the final boundary. This is that which shall arise in the resurrection of the dead.

RECAPITULATION

As someone has said, the Bible begins with a garden and closes with a city. This implies that man need not start over from the beginning. He will not be reduced to infancy when the world is born anew. God will not strike out the history of the world, for he has suffered through it. We share this history with him in suffering, crucifixion, death. Progress will not save anyone, so we need not put our spurs into it in order to approach some form of blessedness. In the Bible, progress assumes the form of a child who becomes a man. But our brother sent from God has been both child and man, and his cross has pierced the entire progression of events from Adam to the Day of Judgment. As a result, there is salvation for our history, and our history will end in a new Jerusalem, filled with a song of love. What prevents us from visualizing this new world is not that it appears so spiritual, so flimsy and logical, but rather that it is permeated by the same mystery which opens a fissure into the heart of our earthly reality — and that this new world is so much richer, that the rainbow over the waterfall in the river of life has so many more colors, and that we shall be able to see them all.

This perspective is not opened up to us by our spirituality, and this heaven cannot be won by our religion. Rather, this is possible because this our day is a part of the history of Jesus Christ — because our time too has been penetrated by his question, "Why hast thou forsaken me?" and by his promise, "It is finished."

II

1. I Am the Root and the Offspring of David

Jesse's Root and Stem

There shall come forth a shoot from the
stump of Jesse,
and a branch shall grow out of his roots.
—Isaiah 11:1

When the prophet wrote these lines, he was thinking of the old royal family and its progenitor, Jesse of Bethlehem. He knew that the axe had been set against the root of the tree, that the time was coming when no more than a stump would remain. But he also knew that a miracle would take place, that a sprout would germinate out of this fragment of life. The Messiah, David's son, would come.

For those of us who believe that Isaiah's prophecy was fulfilled when Jesus was born in Bethlehem, this miracle was not merely a commuted death sentence of an oppressed people, an unexpected renewal of life. When we see Jesus' family tree, as depicted in medieval art, growing out of the sleeping Jesse, or as traced in the Gospel of Matthew, we have reason to wonder that such fruit was produced by such a tree. David's family seems no different from other similar dynasties with respect to war and deceit and guilt. But the new king who appeared in the city of David was different. "And the Spirit of the Lord shall rest upon him," Isaiah continues, "the spirit of wisdom and understanding,/the spirit of counsel and might, /the spirit of knowledge and the fear of the Lord." Thus it was that a new humanity appeared in the midst of the old.

54

Lo, how a Rose e'er blooming
From tender stem hath sprung!
Of Jesse's lineage coming
As men of old have sung.

But that is not all. Faith asserts that this rose is from heaven, God of God, light of light, that the mysterious power off in the distance became a child. An angel, a shepherd from the fields, you or I may perhaps watch over a child one night, somewhere in Bethlehem — and thus come closer to eternity than ever before.

Nevertheless, what the word "Bethlehem" connotes for us is deeply rooted in time and history. How remarkable it is that time should have been fulfilled in such a way, and that history is now "before Christ" and "after Christ."

Like the shepherds of old, who after they had seen the child "returned, glorifying and praising God," so shall we return to the Old Testament, to the time and the world of the prophet "before Christ" when this message was given: "There shall come forth a shoot from the stump of Jesse." All who read the Old Testament with open eyes can recognize themselves in what is here reported. For where have they seen so much cruelty and bitterness before, so many accidents and such immeasurable vanity? They have seen it in their own time and world, in state and church, in culture and economy, in home and society. Humanity "before Christ" lives on in humanity "after Christ." The root and stem are the same. But to return to this after we have been in Bethlehem is not to revert from legend to reality, from a far-distant isle of bliss to our home of sorrow; it is rather to experience one's own world in a new way, as a world in which a miracle has taken place.

Christmas Eve gets its light from something that hasn't happened yet, and in this it is like the Old Testament, as the apostles read it. Its tense is not perfect but future. The entire creation is an Old Testament text, and on the day before

Christmas it reads as follows: This is the earth in which the branch of Jesse has its root. This is the soil in which the miracle was sown. This is the night which is great with the child of heaven. This humanity is the tree which was felled on Judgment Sunday — but a rose shall burst forth from it. And somewhere in space burns a star whose light has not yet reached the earth; it burns, nevertheless, in the darkness that covers us.

The names of many of our flowers bear witness to the midwinter rose produced by the root of Jesse: the Christmas rose, the Christ's-thorn, Our-Lady's-mantle, etc. Further on, Isaiah describes the messianic peace by the figures of animals. He sees the wolf living with the lamb, leopards lying down with kids, and calves and young lions and fattened cattle together. "And," he adds, "a little child shall lead them."

It is as though the fog had lifted from creation and all its agony, enabling us to see what God had intended when he brought it into being. The crucified intention.

We can also see, from this point of view, that the men with whom we quarrel and of whom we speak ill were created for God's peace. If an herb in the field or an ox serves to remind us of the straw and the manger in Jesus' stall, ought we not then to remember the Virgin Mary or Joseph or the child Jesus himself when we meet a man?

But the mystery is still nearer to each one of us than our fellowmen are. It is the mute mystery of the body, which we might have overlooked because of the incense and the angels' song if it hadn't been for the presence of the creatures, resting heavily in their steaming warmth and sleepy sounds — right in the midst of the blessedness of Christmas. This sheer corporeality has stretched like the branch of a root throughout all the ages, man's as well as beast's. Jesse's root and stem.

Thus it is that man in the old covenant also speaks to God about his body: "Thou knowest me right well;/my frame was

not hidden from thee,/when I was being made in secret . . . ./
Thy eyes beheld my unformed substance . . . ." As the fetus
in the womb awaits its day of deliverance, so down through
the years has our corporeality anticipated its adoption, and
God has reckoned its time. This existence "in silence" is God's
root in human life; in nine months the Virgin bore him who
bears up the world.

And while the physical creation reaches out in blind agony
for "the revealing of the sons of God," the soul is sustained by
the prophecies on the long road from Eden's locked gate to
Bethlehem. Songs and visions are soon as numerous as the
stars over the sleeping shepherds. Like a primeval forest they
spread out over the world of men, a primeval forest with its
roots in the subsoil of the soul, nourished by anxiety, with
the crowns of its trees listening to the winds of heaven. There
it is that the gospel of God now grows, a plant from a distant
land, and on this night it blossoms in the wintry woods — a
rose sprung from Jesse's root and stem, God's wisdom blooming
on the root of folly.

To love the cursed earth, man's destiny so bitter and vain,
his sinful body and foolish wisdom. To love the Holy Virgin.

The Name of the Day Is Eve

> "I will put enmity between you and the woman,
>   and between your seed and her seed;
> he shall bruise your head,
>   and you shall bruise his heel."
> To the woman he said,
> "I will greatly multiply your pain in childbearing;
>   in pain you shall bring forth children,
> yet your desire shall be for your husband,
>   and he shall rule over you."
>
> —Genesis 3:15–16

The name of the day is Eve. Just before its beautiful Christmas morn, the church remembers its long night of waiting — the night when the mother of all that lives listens in the darkness. She listens for the danger that lurks in the shadows, the insidious origin of Cain's hate and Abel's death, or the treacherous assault from within, which one day devastated paradise and destroyed the home. Adam's plans, like his foraging expeditions, ranged far and wide. Eve lingered at home and listened. Her enemy was a serpent, a danger in the firewood, a danger within and behind, who crept on the ground and hid under the threshold. And Eve's wisdom has been stored up for a thousand generations; if this weren't so, man would not have been preserved for the hour which was approaching.

What hour? The one in which the serpent's head was bruised. The Scriptures tell us that Eve was right in her enmity. Death did not appear with the roar of the tiger. Evil did not begin with murder and war. Evil thoughts came from the heart. Fires which burned the world were lit at that hearth. And the serpent's downfall shall come from this same source, foretold by the hatred and prayers of women in generation after generation.

This feminine animosity has two faces, one turned down toward the earth where the seed of the serpent crawls and the curse results in death, the other turned toward the new heavens and a new earth, toward the child who will crush the serpent's head. This enmity, in other words, is not simply a psychic peculiarity or a deep-rooted prejudice. From the beginning it has grown together with her "seed," with the child. The child who plays at the reptile's burrow, and then plays no more. The child who carries into the future the promise of the serpent's death. Both malediction and promise are present in the mother from the time the child is conceived in her womb. Enmity and hope. And in the hour of birth, implacable pain and an urgent, blessed longing for the future all join together at a narrow gate, at life's fearful passage of blood and anguish. As Christ said, "When a woman is in travail she has sorrow, because her hour has come; but when she is delivered of the child, she no longer remembers the anguish, for joy that a child is born into the world."

How did Jesus know that? Perhaps this came from what Mary kept and pondered in her heart.

For she who now approaches the city of David, now when the world's clock is being turned back to the night when time was fulfilled — she bears all of the female anguish and longing since the beginning of time. She bears the child who bears the curse in order to abolish it — the child of promise. No angels are present to cast their light on the road she travels, tired and anxiously watching for the light of the inn, for she now knows that her hour is near. There is no room for her there, but she doesn't know it yet. It has been agreed somewhere that she is to experience the agonizing pain of childbirth gradually, as by the spoonful — and also experience the depths of the lovelessness of the life to which her child is to be born and which he is to taste even unto death. She will not only bear this child, with the pains of Eve; she will also, one day, lose it.

According to Revelation, this threat is to take the form of a dragon — as though the serpent of Genesis has grown to assume cosmic proportions in the last book of the Bible. The dragon is a symbol of heaven, and he stands before a woman, waiting for her to give birth to her child.

But this threat is an expression of fear.

The dragon fears neither the great powers, judgments of fire and sword, nor the wrath of the Almighty. But he does fear the child who fulfills the woman's longing. He fears the promise given at the beginning of history, sealed by the special covenant God made with Eve, with Mary, with the church.

What else is there for evil to fear in this world? What enmity can abolish enmity, if not the hatred which God's love has instituted against hatred? Other princes have failed. Other stars have led to calamity. One promise alone remains, carried like a torch through the centuries, from the gates of paradise onward to this stable, not merely as an idea or a dream, but borne in flesh and blood. And finally, God has fulfilled the promise in flesh and blood. Such is the longing of a woman, and the mercy of God in the longest of all nights.

Thus it is that thousands of men and women follow her this night, light-bearers from cities and from desert places. Light the candles, light the torches, light the prayers and the songs of praise. Our mother, with Joseph at her side, shall not go alone through the darkness to Bethlehem. "For . . . to us a son is given; / . . . and his name will be called / 'Wonderful Counselor, Mighty God, / Everlasting Father, Prince of Peace.' "

The woman's sorrow shall bring forth a blessing. The name of the day is Eve. And what was said at the portals of history and what was said when heaven was placed in her womb shall be fulfilled. "Do not be afraid, Mary, for you have found favor with God. And behold, you will conceive in your womb and bear a son, and you shall call his name Jesus."

The Annunciation of Joseph

Now the birth of Jesus Christ took place in this way. When his mother Mary had been betrothed to Joseph, before they came together she was found to be with child of the Holy Spirit; and her husband Joseph, being a just man and unwilling to put her to shame, resolved to divorce her quietly. But as he considered this, behold, an angel of the Lord appeared to him in a dream, saying, "Joseph, son of David, do not fear to take Mary your wife, for that which is conceived in her is of the Holy Spirit; she will bear a son, and you shall call his name Jesus, for he will save his people from their sins." All this took place to fulfil what the Lord had spoken by the prophet:

*"Behold, a virgin shall conceive and bear a son,
and his name shall be called Emmanuel"*

(which means, God with us). When Joseph woke from sleep, he did as the angel of the Lord commanded him; he took his wife, but knew her not until she had borne a son; and he called his name Jesus.

—Matthew 1:18–25

"God is with us" — many battles have been fought with this watchword. Some of these battles have been lost, but the people have experienced a desperate kind of solace as they bowed their necks under the burdens and pains inflicted by the conqueror. "God is with us, God is with us" — a defiant idea with which to persevere.

But one day a command came from the God who had been

so hard to understand; it came out of the somber spaces which separate him from us. A man was sleeping under the cold stars, possessing another kind of space within, equally immeasurable and equally enigmatic. The same mystery spoke out of both depths, and a being of fire took form within; there was fire inside the closed eyelids at this moment, and the sleeping man heard his name: "Joseph, Joseph!" And then, immediately, a significant addition, which foretold what this matter was all about: "son of David!" For this man was the bearer of an historic heritage; he must have been acutely aware of this every time he ventured to say, "God is with us." The nation's hope centered upon this heritage, which was spelled out in the prophecy of Isaiah: "Of the increase of his government and of peace/there will be no end,/upon the throne of David, and over his kingdom . . . ."

But the message took an unexpected turn. It did not deal first of all with the people as a whole; it went straight to the anguish that ached in this man day and night, refusing to leave him even when he slept.This anguish also had a name: "Mary!" Mary was to have a child, and that implied that she belonged to another. This also meant that she was in great danger; her very life might have been in danger, for in the eyes of the law she was already Joseph's wife. Furthermore, the way of escape that Joseph in his confusion had thought of in an effort to save his Jewish honor and his beloved's life had been closed. For the child who was to be born had to belong to the tradition of David; it was a question that concerned the future of the people, and God is with us. It may well be that bitterness began to express itself in Joseph's mind as he slept: "Respect and love and honor mean nothing, apparently; everything must be sacrificed for this David matter!" The Holy Spirit brooded over this new dimension of anguish opened up in Joseph's dreams. A name was called, a name that says that God is salvation. But this was explained in a contradictory way, by saying that *this child* was to save the people, and not from misery and oppression, but from their sins — sins from which only God can save.

It is not entirely clear if the dream ended at this point. The quotation marks found in the translation are not found in the original text. But the passage from Isaiah which is in the background here, the one which reports that a virgin shall bear a son, specifically says "God with us"! Not as a vague hope, but as a personal name. Putting all this together, we find something even more remarkable than the arrival in the world of a new man, perchance a descendant of David. For as John wrote about the child resting in Mary's womb, "He was in the world, and the world was made through him." The birth of a man is a part of creation, but of this man it was said that he was begotten and not made, begotten of the Father in eternity.

This is not so much dogmatics and speculation. If the gospel is correct, this is fact. And if this is right, think for a moment about what it implies: It is no longer a faint hope that God is with us; God is literally here, he is the child of Mary. It is thus that he desires to save the world: through that which is human, through weakness, by waking us up with a child's cry, by disarming us with a child's gesture — arms stretched out toward us. Almighty God saves his people from their sins by loving his way into our world, by filling it in the same way as the child made itself felt in every nerve of Mary's body — a flame within a flame.

Therefore what was sown in weakness, a grain of wheat in human soil, is being sown in congregations of the church today all over the world. The seed comes from love, from salvation, from God. Today the church is Mary, the mother of God. She is part and parcel of sinful humanity, but in the sacrament of the altar he replenishes her with a nearness that is like the nearness of a child. Immanuel.

But what does Joseph say? "Do not fear to take Mary your wife . . . ." How can a man have God in the house without being afraid? Just think of lying awake at night, hearing your wife breathe, and knowing that the world's heart is beating in her womb! The angel was fearsome, but in the presence of him who lay under Mary's heart the angels covered their eyes. "Joseph, son of David, do not fear."

It is this nearness which we have made into a mere detail in our Christmas observance. For his nearness in the gospel is not a pretty picture; it is a nearness equally as earthy and manifest as in Bethlehem or Nazareth. A word on our lips, bread on our table, wine in our flasks. But the angels do not dare look upon him, the worlds quake at his name. Immanuel! What would happen if all those for whom he is a beautiful legend, a sentimental condiment at Christmas, discovered his true identity?

Our text contains a mystery which elicits both a smile and some fear: The Almighty desired Joseph's protection. He lit the stars over Joseph's house, but Joseph had to provide him with a refuge in that house. From this distant God came angels enough to cause Herod's entire army to grow faint; yet they say that Joseph must flee to Egypt for safety, for the government is out to get the child who is David's son!

We know little about Joseph's thoughts; we know him best by what he did. The Joseph of the manger scene is an old man. Many want him that way in order to avoid the idea that the Holy Virgin had other children — as though she would have been less holy as a result! But the Joseph of the Bible took Mary along first of all to Bethlehem, then to Egypt, and from Egypt back to Israel. Could even a refugee family in our time make such a wilderness journey without an excess of strength and determination? So the texts for today refer not only to Mary, the mother, the church. They also speak of Joseph, the descendant of a king, a man of skillful hands, of firm will, of indomitable powers, a guide through unknown lands. The fact that God is with us is not, therefore, just a salubrious concept for those who think we are dealing here with a pretty idea or a childish dream. It summons us to the defense of the gospel.

Joseph could not move a finger to accomplish his salvation; it was the child who saved him from his sins — even though Joseph bore this child in his arms. "If this child had not been born, all flesh would have been lost." God nevertheless desires that we protect this child.

Immanuel! That is salvation by grace alone — but it is not a declaration of irresponsibility. The depth of God's grace opens up new depths to us, that we may serve him by grace. Who will lift the holy flame against the light, and cup his hand around it? Which of us openly confesses the Christmas gospel where it is held in disdain? Who will take the holy sacrament and fight for its honor? Who serves Jesus and his brothers today in roads filled with refugees and in the lumberman's workshop? Who, in Herod's jurisdiction, in alien lands, on the highways and the streets of small towns, will defend this name Jesus?

Not everyone receives a visit from angels, but God's word comes today to many who have been called by name ever since they were baptized. If they listen, one here and one there will hear this word from within as well. God's word frequently speaks through hidden transmitters in the depths of the soul. Anguished dreams and frustrated longings are not alone behind the closed eyes. Among the shadows of perplexity a clear message is sometimes spoken, an appeal of grace. When Joseph awoke, he did as the angel of the Lord had commanded. Some others have also received a command concerning this child, this gospel, this holy name, this mystery of body and blood. When they awake — what will *they* do?

66

Mater Dolorosa

> *Again the Lord spoke to Ahaz, "Ask a sign of the Lord your God; let it be deep as Sheol or high as heaven." But Ahaz said, "I will not ask, and I will not put the Lord to the test." And he said, "Hear then, O house of David! Is it too little for you to weary men, that you weary my God also? Therefore the Lord himself will give you a sign. Behold, a young woman shall conceive and bear a son, and shall call his name Immanuel."*
>
> *—Isaiah 7:10–14*

The Day of the Annunciation almost always falls in Lent. The angel who came to Mary was not the only one who had something to announce. Other powers announce anguish, suffering, death. But what did Mary's angel know about that? The questions which are raised in his conversation with Mary concern a miracle, while the Passion texts are more inclined to ask why no miracles took place. There is no doubt about which kind of question presents the greatest difficulty to faith. Men used to refer to the "why of suffering," often without recognizing that this expression has a dual meaning: the "why" which is spoken in the presence of suffering, and the "why" which suffering itself expresses.

It seems at times that the gospel dwells in two different worlds, the world of Christmas and the world of Good Friday, and that there is no communication between them. Because of this, it is all the more important to speak with a Christmas angel about the "why of suffering." Investigation reveals that the traditional texts for the day of the Annunciation, such as Isaiah 7:10–14, point to this need too.

A king in David's line was once told that two neighboring lands had mobilized and brought their armies together at the border. Then "his heart and the heart of his people shook as the trees of the forest shake before the wind," we read. It was as an answer to such fear that this sign was promised: the young woman should conceive, and her child's time should be a chronological measure for the enemies of Judah. When the child reached the point where he could distinguish between good and evil, their time would expire.

It is the same today. The New Testament answers our uneasy questions with the sign of the annunciation. The church has written this into our solar year, so that our hope has an ally in the passage of time, as the sun and moon and stars continue their celestial excursions. "And a great portent appeared in heaven, a woman clothed with the sun, with the moon under her feet, and on her head a crown of twelve stars; she was with child and she cried out in her pangs of birth, in anguish for delivery."

But the anguish of which our text reminds us today was not a picture in the heavens, a celestial church drama. It was the fate of a woman in Israel.

We should be able to say: a woman's fate similar to many others. It was certainly a long way from Nazareth to Bethlehem, and it must not have seemed particularly strange to give birth in a shed, since no other room could be found. The Evangelist does not complain about this, nor does Mary. The only thing posterity knows of her thoughts at this time is that she "pondered" what had been reported about the angel song which, it was said, had been heard somewhere in that region. Later on — when she was forced to flee with her child — we are told what the exegetes had to say about this matter. But no one remembered to ask what Mary said. Thus it was, all the way to the suffering and death in Jerusalem. Mary witnessed her son's execution; she stood at the cross and heard him cry, "Why?" "Why hast thou forsaken me?" But she herself said nothing. Even her tears went unnoticed — if she had any. It is remarkable therefore that so many unhappy mothers cry out (in the words of Hjalmar Gullberg), "Move over, Mary. There are many of us who need to cry." As though she had said something, or requested some kind of place of honor for her suffering. At the cross, there weren't very many who wanted to join her.

The only "why" which has come down to us from the history of her suffering is the maternal question put to her son the *first* time he was absent for three days without telling her where he was. The *last* time it was perhaps worse, but no "why" has come down to us out of this agony. A sword pierced her soul, but she did not verbalize her torment.

This primitive rock of suffering continues to exist, but no one asks, "Why?" From Eve to Mary the anguish of the child — the anguish of bringing a child into the world and the anguish of losing the child to the world — does not appear with individual nuances. It arises out of our humanity as such, out of existence itself. Here is where the "why" of suffering really enters in. Not a debate about suffering, but suffering's own way of asking the question. The throes of pain shoot in creation: delivery is near. The "why" of suffering is etched into the human body's bloodstained journey — uncompromising as the rush of lemmings, blind as an avalanche of snow — toward the final day. It is etched into the soul's anguish for being itself, its nakedness before God.

Because of this, explanations don't help either. Theories, debates, doctrines do not speak the same language as suffering. Their "therefore" does not answer the "why" of suffering. Like a giant iceberg, agony spreads under the surface. This is one of the reasons why many explanations, Christian and non-Christian, are contradicted everywhere — except where suffering actually exists. Suffering remains silent; it has heard no answer. The panic of Ahaz which reigns in the face of what shall be is a stranger in these parts, as are the moralizing observations of Job's friends, which test the patience of God and man. Both reactions stand in the presence of suffering as if suffering were a meteor which accidentally falls to earth: to them suffering is not one of the elements of life such as air, fire, or water.

When *the sign* comes, the answer to the "why" of suffering, it is no stranger. "And this will be a sign for you: you will find a babe wrapped in swaddling cloths and lying in a manger." This sign was born out of Eve's pain and Mary's anguish. It is to be found outside the security of our lodgings. For "he was despised and rejected . . . ;/a man of sorrows, and acquainted with grief." Mary's son did not go around explaining, but it was our grief that he took upon himself. Neither did he fasten our attention upon his pain — or seek our consoling support. "Don't cry for me." Other answers have been provided, to incline us to relinquish our protests, or to rescue someone's prestige — God's, the church's, the king's, the state's . . . . But *the sign* simply is. Like the signs in the heavens, telling us that a storm is coming. Like the buds on a tree, when summer is nigh. Like a child in its mother's womb.

And this answer is so distant, coming from outside, like an alien skin grafted onto our humanity, that it sometimes seems identical with the question. A ground-shoot emerging from the parched earth. A lamb led away to be slaughtered. The "why" of suffering. Mary's son.

The law and conscience tell us that we have tested God's patience. The prophets said this too. We well know, then, why we suffer. But isn't this also an answer from outside, an inhuman answer? For sin is a "why" also: "I do not understand my own actions." This correlation of sin and suffering, which makes the one a riddle to the other's mother, has not provided us with the answer, only a new "why." And it is before this new "why" that most of the comforters have hestitated. There was Eliphaz, for example, who said in the presence of the suffering Job that "the company of the godless is barren,/and fire consumes the tents of bribery." This reminds us of the time when the venerable apostles asked about the man who was born blind: "Who sinned, this man or his parents?"

But the son of Mary did not stop at this boundary. Not only did he open the eyes of the blind, curb the anguish of the insane, call the dead back to life — and thereby provide thousands upon thousands of clergymen with texts for sermons about sin and repentance. The true dimensions of this forgetfulness are given to us by John the Evangelist, when he points to the sign in the desert and says, "as Moses lifted up the serpent . . . , so must the Son of man be lifted up." And the apostle Paul, when he said of Jesus that he became a curse — yes, even more: he was made sin. Here too, in the human context, question and answer are identical.

Has any kind of answer been given, then? Is not David's son one of us, included with us in Jerusalem, confined within the Aramaean circle? Does the sign indicate *anything besides* the "why" of sin and suffering?

The man born blind thought so; so did the one who regained mastery of himself; so did he who had been dead. But the witness who comes forth is a Virgin who gave birth to a child of David's house. The sign which accompanied this came from the very depths of human life, but also from the heights of divine grace. Cosmic envoys hailed the Virgin with high regard — "Hail Mary!" — and Paul summarized the situation thus: "When the time had fully come, God sent forth his Son, born of woman, born under the law." She was the mother of God.

The answer, therefore, comes from God — and that is not all. God *is* the answer, by virtue of the fact that he so loved the world. His answer can be compared to a mother comforting a child in her arms. Or it can be sensed in the name the Virgin was to give the child: Immanuel. "God with us." God's incarnation is the answer — God's incarnation in suffering, in sin, in death. He gave his answer by being with us.

With us. For when he came to Mary he came to the church, to the world. As the Virgin bore the holy flame in her womb, so does the church bear him through the years. For the gospel in word and sacrament is not a principle, nor a debate, nor an idea. It is as much alive as you and I. It is true man, born of the Virgin Mary. Near us.

To love such a child. Hold eternity in one's arms. Encounter God's smile, the smile of a human child. Comfort Immanuel when someone has struck him. This is to know the nearness of God — as when a child throws its arms around the neck of the one who is comforting it. To be Mary.

For the church to be thus — ought we not then to pronounce our resolutions with a bit more hesitation? Speak out somewhat more quietly? Listen to God's childlikeness? Give ourselves time to be loved by the child who leads wolves and oxen, lions and lambs, into God's green meadows? Bow down and become so small that we can share in God's play on earth, the divine service?

And see him suffer. Not to understand him, but to be with him to the end. Hear the judge pronounce sentence upon him, see the hatred shining in the eyes of the executioners, hear the mob shout, "Crucify, crucify him!"

So the "why" of suffering comes back. It is as when the sword pierced Mary's soul — when the sign was denied and God was sentenced to death. And the mother of this eternal love remained there, near the rejected one, with this pain in body and soul: "Why must God suffer?"

No, we will have no dogmatic analysis now. We ask to be excused from pretentious explanations. Perhaps we should wish the same for God, on this day of the incarnation — and permit the question to sink down into Mary's secret. Down into the depths of humanity, where God so loves, God so loves. If we suffer with him, we shall also be glorified with him.

Heaven Comes to Galilee

In the sixth month the angel Gabriel was sent from God to a city of Galilee named Nazareth, to a virgin betrothed to a man whose name was Joseph, of the house of David; and the virgin's name was Mary. And he came to her and said, "Hail, O favored one, the Lord is with you!" But she was greatly troubled at the saying, and considered in her mind what sort of greeting this might be. And the angel said to her, "Do not be afraid, Mary, for you have found favor with God. And behold, you will conceive in your womb and bear a son, and you shall call his name Jesus.

> He will be great, and will be called the Son of the Most High;
> and the Lord God will give to him the throne of his father David,
> and he will reign over the house of Jacob for ever;
> and of his kingdom there will be no end."

And Mary said to the angel, "How can this be, since I have no husband?" And the angel said to her,

> "The Holy Spirit will come upon you,
> and the power of the Most High will overshadow you;
> therefore the child to be born will be called holy, the Son of God.

And behold, your kinswoman Elizabeth in her old age has also conceived a son; and this is the sixth month with her who was called barren. For with

HEAVEN COMES TO GALILEE

*God nothing will be impossible." And Mary said,
"Behold, I am the handmaid of the Lord; let it be
to me according to your word." And the angel departed from her.*

—Luke 1:26–38

Some of you may be wondering how I can now avoid
talking about the Virgin Birth. I have no intention of even
trying to avoid this, and for two reasons: one, because the
text refers to it, and two, because I believe it. But Luke's
reason for mentioning this and my reasons for believing it
do not "prove" that such a thing is possible. Like us, the
Virgin Mary wondered about this, but the Evangelist does not
present any comprehensive discussion of the matter. In many
countries, when the pastor reads these words in our oldest
creed: "came down from heaven, and was incarnate by the
Holy Ghost of the Virgin Mary, and was made man," it is
customary for him to bow in reverence. All of the authors in
the New Testament do the same when they touch upon the
mystery of the Incarnation. I desire to do this too, not because
the mystery goes beyond my powers of reason, but because
behind the words of Luke I can glimpse the vastest perspective
I know. My mind is not at all forbidden to enter here, but
when it does, it is caught up in God's love for the world, and
this is a well which has no bottom.

The angel which appeared in the streets of Nazareth was
not some kind of Sancta Lucia in a nightgown, carrying white
lilies, as is sometimes depicted; he was a cosmic prince! In
Daniel we are told that the prophet lost consciousness when
he met this ambassador from heaven — and here, all of a
sudden, he stood in a little room where a young girl was
scrubbing the floor, or whatever she was doing at the time.
One of God's seven ministers greeted Mary in a small town.
In that land men never greeted women — not even their

75

betrothed. Small wonder "she was greatly troubled at the saying, and considered in her mind what sort of greeting this might be."

We get some idea of "what this might be" from the fact that the angel quoted the Old Testament. A Messiah shall be born. A mixed variety of dreams, some concerning political power, others concerning heaven and eternity, shimmer in these words. But at last a virgin shall give birth to a child, as Isaiah foretold, a child who was to be known as "God with us."

But there is a hidden meaning in all of this, an unusual double exposure which enables us to discern something of greater significance behind the image of Jacob's house and David's throne and an imperishable dream-kingdom. The fabric has features that were not woven on a man-made shuttle. What was announced was not a new combination of earthly threads — as when a man is conceived. That which was foretold was not simply a new wave rising on the sea of humanity, emerging from heritage and history. The restraint characteristic of this report is reminiscent of the wings of the seraphim, behind which they conceal their faces. But this modesty is not of the kind that often accompanies human conception; the Bible is not devious about such matters. And the idea that sex is rather more "dirty" than human life in general, and must therefore be eliminated in connection with the birth of the *holy* child — such an idea may be typical of modern times, but it would be preposterous in the biblical context. No, the circumstances surrounding the Incarnation were light-years removed from such heresy.

One circle of the light emanating from the divine unity was about to break away. One of the three who constitute eternal love was ready to lose himself in the depths of the human sea. The Son, the Image, the living mirror in which the Creator expressed himself before there was such a thing

as space, was to fall down like a star or a glistening coin —
to fall into the dust of this land that we call history. "The
child to be born" is not the product of a human embrace; he
was before the creation, he was God from all eternity, but
he was not always man. It is now possible for man to think
that God in some way involved himself in a human achieve-
ment when it reached its zenith and, so to speak, approached
the level of the superhuman — just as a man may sometime
imagine that he has touched God while enraptured by a work
of art. But when God threw himself down into our human
world, it was not like an electric arc over something especially
attractive in a great man's life, nor like a poetic blessing
over some great moment in time — an infatuation, a victory,
a hero's death. I restrain myself when I say that, and I cannot
help wondering if the power of the word has beguiled me,
but this, one must assert, is the meaning of the gospel: God
became man. He was bound first of all not in Gethsemane
but in Nazareth. He was fettered first of all not by rope but
by human blood. Long before he was confined in the court
of the high priest, he was confined by human destiny. The
nails used on the cross were there from the beginning, for
so it was that he was nailed to that which is human, and he
could not forsake us. At the time when these controversial
words were inserted into the Apostles' Creed — "conceived by
the Holy Spirit, born of the Virgin Mary" — there was no
question concerning the divinity of Jesus Christ. But what
men wanted to express was that his humanity is humanity
to its very roots and sources. His heaven was at one time an
earthly mother's womb. That within us which refuses to accept
this is not the modern conception of what is possible and
impossible, but our faith in greatness. It is blasphemous to
think that God could have been so little. Even our religious
faith finds it difficult to get away from the pagan idea that
sin resides in the flesh, and that this separates us from God.

That the divine word became flesh is the great stumbling block in our gospel.

We are alienated from God by our ineradicable worship of the gods we have fabricated out of lofty ideas and noble offices. This hierarchical system was offended when Gabriel had to bow before the young girl in Nazareth. When God was born as a Jew and was thenceforth known as a "Nazarene," the order which sorts humanity out into princes and slaves was broken. It was broken by a love which compels the prince of all princes to be the slave of all slaves. As when someone loses himself in the one he loves. As when a mother plunges into a burning house to be with her child. As when an artist sells that last thing he owns in order to make something which has no market value. Such was the passion which flung God down into a mother's womb.

Therefore I shall no longer seek him in the heights. What unites us is not lofty spiritual experience, not the good fortune which many point to as proof that God is with us, not the advantages which distinguish me from the godless masses. That kingdom which has no end is anchored in world history, because it is human. Names such as Jacob and David stand out like rugged boulders, firmly fixed in realities which are recognized not only by prophets and priests but also by politicians and social workers. The kingdom of which we speak is constructed on this history — for David's son was banished by the Herod who is called the Great, and finally suffered under Pontius Pilate. "Finally" — but the kingdom did not end with this suffering and death. The gospel has broken through all hindrances and has reached down to me where I am now standing. It comes, as Gabriel came into a humble home in a small town, to greet man in the midst of his concerns. The bread and wine which at one time graced a heavenly banquet at a wayside in Galilee also belong to my realities. For the bread on the altar is not only of the fields on which a sower has sown; it is also a product of modern industry. Contemporary commerce and politics and social conflict are also brought to the altar where the flame which was lighted in Nazareth continues to burn. Everything is incorporated into his kingdom, for after all he came as a man, not merely as a spirit.

To be sure, the stars are now dim over Bethlehem, and the God who spoke there has hidden his face. But I seek him, not in the cipher code of life and destiny, but in the man from Nazareth. This Jew, this gospel, this bread. The God who reveals his power in the fact that he is so human, and his majesty in the fact that he has stepped down into my poverty, was born of the Virgin Mary. Because of this gift of love, the devil of human superiority has been exorcised, and God is with us. As a result, I approach the message of the man from Nazareth with a certain reserve, for he is Mary's son; he speaks her dialect and shares her primitive world view. The Omniscient speaks through his limitations. And the bread which is broken in his name is heaven in my hand — I wonder that I don't burn my fingers. This is God. And the love I see in this face is nearly terrifying in its greatness, not least because it became so utterly impoverished. For with God nothing is impossible.

Among those who believe that they believe, there often exists a peculiar anxiety about how they will fare, how "things will go" with them. What others say about them and how well they succeed are of prime importance. That is human, but it isn't faith, not the Christian faith. "If God is for us, who is against us?" So said Paul, who did not look to "success" to prove that God was with him. He looked to the miracle from Nazareth, "the love of God in Christ," as he called it. If it is true that Christ has come to us in this way, perhaps man ought not to place such emphasis upon the vicissitudes of fortune. Fear not! Even our sins do not have the right to terrorize us. Therefore repent and confess them, and thus find reason for believing in something even more remarkable: the fact that our sins could not prevent God from coming to us as man.

To us. To whom exactly? It is customary in the Christian tradition to find Old Testament parallels to New Testament figures. The Virgin Mary has not found a counterpart in a queen or in a female prophet. She does not belong exclusively either to the great or to the godly. Men have referred to her as the second Eve. Mary is also the mother of all, for she gave birth to him who is brother to all. And *his* kingdom shall have no end, even though others have. All barriers are broken. Because God has come to us as man, neither the spiritual nor the nonspiritual can imprison him in spirituality. Because a mother's womb became his heaven, one cannot have him to oneself in a heaven which excludes the human element, and one cannot feel safe from him by ignoring heaven and interesting oneself only in what is earthly. He has never permitted himself to be confined either in Jacob's house or in any other house, not even in heaven. And to the extent that I draw a barbed wire around my kind, my spirituality, or my worldliness, in order to be something special before God, I separate myself from Christ.

If it is true that we possess him in the gospel, then it is also true that the gospel is for everyone, wherever one is, whatever one is. If it is true that we possess him in the Lord's Supper, then it is also true that the way to the altar is open to all who hunger. May they come! The disciples have to make room, as on that occasion when people came to Jesus with their children, that he might bless them. The church is open, the godly and the ungodly fences are broken. God is come in humanity, and his kingdom will never end.

The Prophecy of Heaven, the Earth, and My Heart

> *"And now men cannot look on the light*
> *when it is bright in the skies,*
> *when the wind has passed and cleared them.*
> *Out of the north comes golden splendor;*
> *God is clothed with terrible majesty."*
> —Job 37:21–22

This is a description of nature. Job's friend, Elihu, is asking if we have not seen the light which emanates from all creation because it was brought into being by God. He reminds us of the clarity of the heavens when the clouds suddenly break. We experience something similar to this when the first snow falls, or when a large, tree-surrounded lake freezes over. In the next chapter of Job we read this: "From whose womb did the ice come forth,/and who has given birth to the hoarfrost of heaven?/The waters became hard like stone,/and the face of the deep is frozen." To him who has eyes to see, all of this is a miracle: the solidity of stone is just as remarkable as that of ice, and when gravel suddenly appears under melting ice in the spring thaw, we are quite astonished to be reminded once again that such things exist.

But when one sees this luster, like that of a work fresh from the artist's hand, one can also perhaps discern a change caused by suffering. "We know," says Paul, "that the whole creation has been groaning in travail together until now."

These signs are probably most obvious in those events which break the ordinary run of things. A nation is about to die of thirst in the desert; but the leader strikes a rock, which then bursts and produces a spring of water. Or a man agonizes through a night because he is compelled to make a fateful decision. He prays for a sign, and lays an armful of freshly clipped wool on the ground; in the morning, the ground is dry, but the man is able to squeeze enough dew out of the wool to fill an entire bowl. Even an ox or an ass, seeking to find its way home in the twilight, bears mute testimony to the way creatures suffer, to a kind of longing for home in the soil itself. And when the cranes fly north, or when the pond reflects a star, then man can read the signs and perceive that he lives in a prophecy: "And now men cannot look on the light/when it is bright in the skies."

Tonight, a man and woman seek a room; they are tense, for her hour is near. It is written that at such a time a woman is in alliance with all of the marks of creation; yes, she bears them on her own body. The luster and agony of life have gathered in these months, in these days, in this moment. With pain shall she give birth to her child of longing.

But this night is not only the epitome of all prophecy, man's and nature's; it is also the fulfillment. Not because the world's longing has found its home, but because the home of the world has come to dwell in that longing. The primordial fire which shone in creation's morn and which brought about the miracle of existence — this fire has assumed human form. God has become the child of Mary. Thus it is that the Word which created has become a part of its creation. This is the answer to all questions, and the solution to the mysterious cipher. This is the kind of answer that love provides. It is not an explanation of everything, but a presence in everything.

It was because of this, therefore, that the rock burst and that Gideon's wool was damp with dew. It is because of this that the stars are reflected in the eye of the pond. It is because of this that the ox and the ass know what it is to long for the manger and stall. The longing which is found in everything is a mysterious certainty, a certainty related to Mary's hour, a certainty about Jesus Christ.

And the angels, those invisible cosmic powers, the angels of the people, the angels of the forests and the deserts, the angels of space and stars — all come forth out of their darkness and sing. The rocks sing, the springs sing, the stars sing. We also sing.

I speak as though this were happening at this very moment, and someone may think that this is some kind of Christmas play. As though the story of Mary and Joseph and the child Jesus were a legend. But it is not a legend; it is the gospel. And in the gospel time is suspended, the past is the present. This is explained by the fact that the gospel is God's word, which is eternal. In this gospel, each city and village becomes Bethlehem, and each church that manger. This is no play; it is fearfully serious — and at the same time it is a great joy.

Ever since God's word became man the earth has borne this presence, which is like the presence of a child in a woman's womb. Now humanity travels the long road to Bethlehem and to the night when the heavens once again burst over the earth. But the presence which now makes its appeal with the voice of the gospel, an appeal like that of a child or of someone searching for a place to stay, shall then be the presence of unconcealed majesty, permeating everything in heaven and earth like cosmic radiation. "And now men cannot look on the light/when it is bright in the skies . . . ;/God is clothed with terrible majesty."

We approach the holy land. It is like traveling by airplane; one must stay to the end of the journey; one can't step out. But at long last the destination can be seen, like a jewel down in the depths, and a sign flashes, telling us to get ready. So shall it be with creation's homecoming, that for which everyone has been longing.

For this reason Christians pray, in an ancient Christmas collect, that "as they rejoice in the advent of thine only-begotten Son according to the flesh, so when he cometh a second time in his Majesty, they may receive the reward of eternal life." Christmas is a serious matter! Through it eternity has come into time, into our own time. Eternity — and the security that we and all creation seek in anguish. And over the things of this earth we see more clearly the luster of the love which has created them and called them to itself. The source of light itself burns in our midst this night. Mary's child, God of God, light of light. The Word from the book and the altar. Can men look upon this light? "We have beheld his glory," answers the Evangelist, "glory as of the only Son from the Father," full of "grace and truth."

We Shall Have a Child

> *For to us a child is born,*
>   *to us a son is given;*
> *and the government will be upon his shoulder,*
>   *and his name will be called*
> *"Wonderful Counselor, Mighty God,*
>   *Everlasting Father, Prince of Peace."*
>
> —Isaiah 9:6

In the beginning it was a question concerning an event at the Jewish court, some news with important social and political consequences. Seven centuries later the message had become a venerated religious text, a beautiful old poem to recite at ceremonious occasions: "To us a child is born . . . ."

But one day this message exploded in the land like a rusty mine from a long-forgotten war. Here, long afterwards, it sounds like the collision of one legend with another. This reaction is conditioned by the dust of time, by the countless seconds that form a fine layer of powder over that which happened. In our day we set it in Gothic type and delight in the ancient sounds, or, what is worse, we wrap it all up in smooth, sentimental phrases. Sometimes the romance of Christmas seems to depend upon something other than mere distance in time and place. It depends on the *desire* to be distant, as though we prefer to give the illusion that the gospel is an illusion. Let us take a good hold of the dust mop and see what this text really says: "We shall have a child."

An angel spoke with a young girl in Nazareth. This reference to angels is especially comforting to those who finally decide that this is nothing but a harmless legend. But these angelic confrontations were not just so much Christmas-tree tinsel to the persons involved.

Not for Mary. For the following nine months the message from on high continued to grow, both as rumor and as anguish: Mary is going to have a child! Until that difficult hour arrived in the dark cattle shed, what did Mary know about Bethlehem other than that it was a long way from home? That it was inhospitable was something she was to learn by personal experience.

The angel's message did not bring Joseph any special kind of serenity either. "Joseph, son of David, do not fear to take Mary your wife . . . ." That was easy to say, but when has a heavier burden ever been placed upon a carpenter? And the next angel said, "Rise, take the child and his mother, and flee to Egypt . . . ." The Joseph of the Christmas crèche knows nothing about this; he doesn't have to pay taxes, or declare bankruptcy. His role, down through the centuries, has been to pose in the crèche with the ox and the ass. What does he care about affairs in Nazareth? . . . But the Joseph who was the son of David was subjected to one test after the other. On top of everything else, he ran the risk of being misunderstood by the political leaders, involved as he was in a messianic adventure. And there is nothing to indicate that the attitude of the authorities was improved by the fact that Joseph was obliged to flee to Egypt.

We shall have a child. But we have made the angels into cute Christmas-tree decorations. We have camouflaged Mary's suffering by the use of tawdry art forms. We have falsified Joseph into a nice little papa—a bit religious, certainly, but . . . doesn't he look a lot like St. Nicholas? The holy family has become a commercial interest of the first order; it legitimizes the year's greatest orgy in food and luxuries and extravagance. And when everything reaches its culmination we make the old prophecy into a Christmas flag to be placed at the very top of the tree: "To us a child is born."

But at a bus stop on a busy street, surrounded by gaudy display windows and costly Christmas decorations, the Holy Virgin stands, pressed in the crowd. She is waiting for a bus which has room for her and the child she has with her in a carriage. She is a refugee. Her husband is standing in a line somewhere seeking permission to work. At that very moment, a hundred pastors are pondering the message they are to give about the child sleeping there in the carriage. It says in their texts that this child is God. This is a fantastic assertion, but it is even more fantastic to point out that this is why we celebrate Christmas — such a Christmas.

Bustle and finery, in the Christmas context, represent a flight from reality. Such terms as "Christmas snow" and "Christmas candles" reflect this falsity. God is not the only refugee here; we too are in flight. We are running from a God whom we cannot manipulate, from the fact that a child has been born to us. The entire merry-go-round serves to silence the gospel which says that God was born somewhere on the shady side and that he belongs to our family. Thus it is that we avoid seeing and hearing what goes on next door to our comfortable affluent society, and how this concerns us in some way, like a child we have received. This God who is haunted by hunger and by the executioner, who is the very center of our existence (if the gospel is right), is the God whom we have successfully installed in a display window. We have shut him out once again, and now we stand looking at the result through the glass.

But perhaps it is we, and not our God in the baby carriage, who have been deserted by reality. We are mechanical dolls, living in a toyland with buses and trains and cotton snow.

Beyond the bright lights stands reality, reflecting upon the scene. The child has come to us. God and all the angels. And God's hungry brothers and sisters.

On occasion a hole appears in the display, and some of us tumble out into the darkness and the other reality. It seems that Christmas is a mockery "in such a world." We feel as though we are "on the outside." But it is such who can grasp the meaning of the Christmas gospel. For we are where the child is, the one who has been given to us. Beyond illusion. Near to God.

II

2. The Bright Morning Star

God's Journey

> *In those days a decree went out from Caesar Augustus that all the world should be enrolled. This was the first enrollment, when Quirinius was governor of Syria. And all went to be enrolled, each to his own city. And Joseph also went up from Galilee, from the city of Nazareth, to Judea, to the city of David, which is called Bethlehem, because he was of the house and lineage of David, to be enrolled with Mary, his betrothed, who was with child.*
>
> —Luke 2:1–5

These chronological facts have been discussed in a lively way by research scholars. Both Quirinius and the enrollment are well known. The difficulty is to make Luke's data correspond with those of Matthew, who tells us that Jesus was born during the reign of King Herod. We shall not involve ourselves in this debate now. We shall merely note it and then proceed.

Legends do not elicit such debates; neither do dreams or myths. Scholars do not carry on discussions about who reigned when Snow White was with the dwarfs, or when the goddess Athena sprang forth from her father's head. This is not only because these stories are so improbable, or because people no longer believe that they ever took place. Whether these legends or myths can be made into history is not essential; they are just as good apart from such confirmation.

The same holds true with respect to many religions. They are as timeless as dreams or as the floating clouds. Their gods reflect the natural cycle or minister to spiritual needs which remain the same from age to age. No one asks when they were born; they have no history. For their adherents, time is a surging sea. Historical events leave no enduring results; they are like storms and the sun, which fail to etch anything upon the surface of the sea.

And we — what are time and history to us? When we wish each other a merry Christmas, aren't we doing the same as those who practice the religions of nature, even though we reckon in terms of materials other than game and ground nuts? Aren't our wishes also a symbolic accumulation of all that is included in "doing well"? Legendary figures from pre-Christian epochs return. Santa Claus has gone through many transformations, but he is obviously an old fertility god. We must not be confused by the fact that he appears on TV, his blessings packaged in such a modern way. Technology doesn't change anything. There he sits in his sleigh, nearly buried by gifts, the god of plenty proclaiming the ancient message of success and well-being as the meaning of life.

I am not saying this in order to warn you about Santa Claus. But if our society has in fact come to trust in him, it is all the more necessary for us to be reminded that our festival of life actually has been given a dimension that is different from this annual repetition of the rites of extravagance. We are no longer "nature people"; we now have a history. In the midst of the primitive, monotonous feast of plenty rings the voice of the Evangelist. He does not say, "Once upon a time," and he does not permit the snow of legend to fall upon his message. He asserts, pungently and factually, that "a decree went out from Caesar Augustus . . . when Quirinius was governor of Syria. . . . And Joseph also went up from . . . Nazareth, to Judea, to the city of David, which is called Bethlehem, because he was of the house and lineage of David . . . ."

It must have seemed presumptuous for Luke to mention such well-known men as Augustus and Quirinius in order to document the chronological context within which Mary and Joseph undertook their journey. But when Christianity came to recognize the implications of what he reported, it was this journey which became, instead, the point of orientation used to date Augustus and Quirinius. That these men are remembered at all is due chiefly to the fact that they are involved in this story.

Names and values come and go; like vegetation and insects, they have their appointed times. Our cultures and nations shall one day be forgotten. Researchers may puzzle over certain bits of plastic — that material seems to be the most durable of all we have contrived — discovered where Stockholm or New York once stood. But at that time men shall read, in churches we are unable to visualize, and in languages we do not know: "In those days a decree went out from Caesar Augustus . . . ."

For humanity's destiny has been given a common denominator. Existence involves more than merely to exist. Life on our planet has become a drama. The monotonous repetition of events has at one point been pierced. Something has happened.

When we hear this message in the midst of our festivities, Christmas takes on meaning. And Christmas is, in reality, an epitome of all years and all epochs. In Christmas all of life takes on meaning. It has become history.

And what is this all about? It concerns the fact that God became man. He did not remain in the hidden, out of which the gifts of creation come: rain and sun and grain. He himself became a part of creation, and this journey provided the course of world events with an axle on which to turn. "He came to his own home, and his own people received him not. But to all who received him, who believed in his name, he gave power to become children of God." It is therefore not *by this* that time becomes history, that human destiny is given a face, that all receive him and talk about him. If all were to reject him, that too would be a part of this dramatic event. If God became unfashionable, that would be a catastrophe — for that which is fashionable.

But if everything has to do with this journey which began in Nazareth and ended at Golgotha, how does this tie in with the "other Christmas," with well-being and with wonderland?

In the first place, we now know how to distinguish between pretense and reality. We have been provided with a defense against commercialism, and we realize that what is really important is not to be found in a display window. We have also learned to know that all gifts are worthless if they are not given in love. No longer can we find comfort in anonymous consignments. Since love came into the world, we are not so easily deceived by affluence. There must be someone to thank — and to thank for more than gifts — if prosperity is not to look like poverty.

In the second place, God's journey poses questions that are concerned precisely with our abundance. And that come to us through our abundance. If we answer *by giving,* we answer correctly. But at the same time we are confronted by two new questions. What is behind our gifts? And do they ever go *to those who need them the most?* For as a result of that which happened in Nazareth and Bethlehem, abundance and undernourishment have ceased to be private, unrelated concerns.

Thus it is that each of us, and our whole era, has been drawn into something bigger than the question of whether or not we are prosperous; they have been drawn into the drama of divine love. We have received power to become the children of God, to become the brother of Jesus Christ and his brothers — and also to say no to our own history by trying to live as though we are not his contemporaries. We find ourselves at a fork in the road between Nazareth and Bethlehem. As the Mother of God comes down the road, heavy in her ninth month, we are called out of our wonderland of irresponsibility, called to reality as it is in Christ.

God in Our Possession

In those days a decree went out from Caesar Augustus that all the world should be enrolled. This was the first enrollment, when Quirinius was governor of Syria. And all went to be enrolled, each to his own city. And Joseph also went up from Galilee, from the city of Nazareth, to Judea, to the city of David, which is called Bethlehem, because he was of the house and lineage of David, to be enrolled with Mary, his betrothed, who was with child. And while they were there, the time came for her to be delivered. And she gave birth to her first-born son and wrapped him in swaddling cloths, and laid him in a manger, because there was no place for them in the inn.

And in that region there were shepherds out in the field, keeping watch over their flock by night. And an angel of the Lord appeared to them, and the glory of the Lord shone around them, and they were filled with fear. And the angel said to them, "Be not afraid; for behold, I bring you good news of a great joy which will come to all the people; for to you is born this day in the city of David a Savior, who is Christ the Lord. And this will be a sign for you: you will find a babe wrapped in swaddling cloths and lying in a manger." And suddenly there was with the angel a multitude of the heavenly host praising God and saying,

"Glory to God in the highest,
and on earth peace among men with whom he is
        pleased!"

When the angels went away from them into heaven, the shepherds said to one another, "Let us

> *go over to Bethlehem and see this thing that has*
> *happened, which the Lord has made known to us."*
> *And they went with haste, and found Mary and*
> *Joseph, and the babe lying in a manger. And when*
> *they saw it they made known the saying which had*
> *been told them concerning this child; and all who*
> *heard it wondered at what the shepherds told*
> *them. But Mary kept all these things, pondering*
> *them in her heart. And the shepherds returned,*
> *glorifying and praising God for all they had heard*
> *and seen, as it had been told them.*
>
> —Luke 2:1–20

After Joseph lifted the latch from the door of the stall, Mary walked heavily over the floor. Was there a bit of straw to rest upon? Her hour had come, the inevitable from which there was no turning back.

Yes, she who is with child must give birth, and he who is born must get on with that which is human. The inexorable cannot be escaped. The angels looked with terror upon the way in which the only-begotten Son entered upon this fate. He became man, and as such could not escape anything, neither hunger nor thirst, neither loneliness nor disappointment, neither defeat nor the merriment of evil forces. And at the end of the road the cross was waiting; nothing that he said or prayed could change that. He had to choose either the cross or treachery, and it is hard to say which was the worse.

That was a dark night, a night when a human birth took place in the midst of great suffering, but also in the midst of angels' songs. I do not believe that anyone heard a sweet little Christmas carol. I rather believe that on that night the entire universe shook as it will only one more time — at the end of the world. A cry of amazement and perplexity rang through the heavens that night, for God was now no longer above and beyond the vicissitudes of life. His heart was now bound and held in the human, and even his power and majesty could not alter this situation. For from this moment he was where this child was, laughing and suffering with mankind down in an out-of-the-way place on a small, whirling speck of dust among a myriad of other specks in the cosmos.

What happens if this love is rejected? What if the Lord of heaven stands as a beggar before the door, and no one opens? It is somewhat astounding to think that man, who had suffered so under the compulsion to live and the compulsion to die, now came to have power over the Lord of life and death. He came as a little child, in our possession. Man was given the opportunity to determine *his* fate, just as *he* has determined ours. If he did not have such power we would live in fear of what might happen to us. Good and bad fortune overtake us, and we take the one as well as the other. Sometimes we desire to rise in opposition, but that serves no purpose. And then, all of a sudden, man has control over God, for God is a little child in Bethlehem, and man can turn him away from the inn. What freedom, what terrible fredom! The heavens must fear for God's own fate, the universe must quake before the will of man, which now is lord over God himself.

But the earth too quakes before the will of man. King David, on one occasion, had to choose between falling into God's hands or into man's, and he chose the former. Modern man has the key to powers of which our fathers were unaware. He holds sway over matter's own secret, and in our own time there is no greater cause for fear. The more we ponder our history the more clearly we can see that we are our own worst enemies, that the greatest bitterness always arises out of the bitterness of our own hearts. We covet control of our own destiny, and nothing is more dangerous than success in this. At one time God was in the hands of man, and man's will was the lot of the only-begotten Son. But we want to pray: "Save us from ourselves."

Nevertheless, there was joy too in the heavenly song that rang out over Bethlehem. For God's weakness before the men who caused him to knock at the door of their inn is more powerful than all the Milky Ways. When God stepped into human destiny and submitted himself to the compulsions of birth and life and death, this meant that thenceforth he was to dwell in darkness as well as in light. Heaven has been mortgaged by the very fact that it was relinquished, and for many it is easier to find heaven outside the closed doors of fortune than it is within. The presence of hell on earth no longer goes unchallenged, for God has placed a cross in the midst of the power of evil, and there he himself suffers with us, there he forms a paradise for the penitent thief. Some have not found that the shame and suffering of their own crosses have been reduced by this. It is still no picnic to bear a child in poverty. But because we rediscover the meaning of our lives in Christ we can dare to believe, even when things are at their worst, that God has set his heaven in reality.

God has come into our world with a heaven that death cannot destroy. When he gave himself into our possession, it was not in some passive way, but in the dynamics of love. The Lord of the universe lay as a child at the human breast. Man can close his eyes to the heavenly majesty, he can defy laws and threats and punishment and death — but how can he close his heart to a child who wails in the darkness? A child's hand has grabbed hold of man's coat — is there anything stronger? So it was that God loved the world.

We pray, "Deliver us from evil," and we think of what the world calls powerful: we think of cruel fate, we think, perhaps mostly, of ourselves. "Save us from ourselves." In the Christmas gospel our prayer is heard. He who is the Lord in the city of David is the answer to prayer.

Glory to God in the highest, and on earth peace, goodwill toward men.

Our God in the Straw

> *"And this will be a sign for you: you will find a babe wrapped in swaddling cloths and lying in a manger."*
>
> —Luke 2:12

After all visions and miracles, after suns have been lighted and have expired, after heroes and prophets have come and gone, their kingdoms sunk in oblivion, this sign remains to us. The child — not something especially angelic or heavenly, but a human child like those who millions of times have delighted their mothers — and also disturbed their sleep. A child who slept with his hands up alongside his head and who made sucking noises with his hungry mouth. But there was something which distinguished him from other children, enabling us to see that this was God who lay there and slept. That something was the manger. Only God could be so poor under a broken heaven. And the great marvel is not heaven, but the poverty of earth. If the gospel is right, only God can be sufficiently human to get to the bottom of our despair. Is it right?

In any case, it is right in telling us what it is to be human when chance and the pretty legends have been pruned away, what it is to be excluded, to be defenseless in the dark, to be subjected to a fate like the one that marked this child from the very beginning. Legends are the things we believe when we illumine our homes and celebrate our plans, our victories, our decisions. When we hold our meetings, increase the tempo of our work, and intensify our economic calculations, we appear with a romantic veneered surface that encases our well-being and glistens with lofty sentiments. But in this night the veneer was shattered, enabling us to see reality. And this is the sign, which is understood by those who need it: that the gospel has its roots precisely in this place; yes, that the Word became reality where this fissure opened up and this truth emerged; that this child, who is said to be God, lay wrapped in the manger of our poverty.

This does not mean that the gospel works with pretty pictures of our situation, though one has to say that it might gain a foothold in our confidence in this way. Neither do we find this idea in philosophical systems or in imposing speculations. That God would come to us in such a manner is an offense against everything that we have imagined about God. The matter possesses the credibility of incredibility, and that is no ordinary credibility.

And when we observe that the depths of humanity were opened up, not by a crowbar of trial and judgment, but by a groping hand which seeks to find us, by a child who was given into our possession, then we may well reflect upon this in our hearts and ask ourselves if the gospel is not right after all in saying that only God could be so human.

If this is true, then lonesomeness and the curse of being human have vanished, for God has chosen to dwell with the excluded and to unite himself with our dark fate. Then it is that you can hear his breath as you stand outside where perplexity dwells — if only you have the gospel with you. Much surrounds us this night, and not all of it makes us joyful, much less secure. But the nearness of the child is also evident; whose presence is more obvious? The sound of a marching army cannot be heard more clearly than the crying of a child. And this is a real child, not a doll or a product of fantasy; the swaddling cloths are mentioned as proof. We can be sure that there were diapers hanging outside when the wise men came. And his nearness is just as inescapable today as it was in Bethlehem. If you are very quiet you will hear him breathe, just as Mary did when she sat up to listen and found that he was indeed alive, that everything was true. You will also see that the gospel is alive, whenever it is read in unadorned realities and unromanticized darkness. Perhaps this can be seen even more clearly when the table is set for those who journey in the darkness, and the Word takes form in the bread and wine of our poverty, with the church serving as his stall and the altar as his manger.

But if it is true that God is with us in weakness, what weakness can then separate us from him? If he lights his candle in those places where the journey is most difficult, what hardships can then separate us from him? And how could the destruction of the temple take from us a God whom we recognize because he dwelt in a stall and lay swaddled in a manger?

"And this will be a sign for you." There is no other. Some have expected to find the sign in us; perhaps you have expected that yourself—as if certain believers had qualities that could elicit our confidence. But the truth of the matter is well summed up in the words we use when we confess our sin.

That God came to Bethlehem, such as it was, and to the place where you are now, such as it is, is a sign that we shall find, not in the heights of our fancy, but in the humanity of a newborn child lying in the straw of our poverty.

God in the Hours of Night

> When the angels went away from them into heaven, the shepherds said to one another, "Let us go over to Bethlehem and see this thing that has happened, which the Lord has made known to us."
> —Luke 2:15

We often desire this very thing: to be able to see. To have God proven to us in such a way as to remove all doubt. To feel his grace so surely that we would know we possessed it. To have his mighty deeds explained so that we could understand their hidden meanings.

Let us go over to Bethlehem and see. But if we did get to see all the angels the shepherds saw, what would we have accomplished? We would have proven the existence of the spiritual world. But what good would that do? Isn't evil a spiritual thing too? And the devil? And if we did hear the heavenly song in our hearts, what would that do for us? We could probably call that peace, but how could we be sure that this was peace with God? Can't the heart lie? And what do we accomplish with what we call explanations? Explanations do not help those who long for love.

Thus it was that God himself came instead of providing us with proof and explanations, something to remember. Let us go to Bethlehem and see. But see what? A child in the straw, a word in the book, some bread on the table. For what the shepherds went to see was the same as that which we have come to see: "And the Word became flesh and dwelt among us." They left the place where the angels and the heavenly glory had shone around them in order to see something greater: a stable, a child, a manger. This proves nothing to either pious or worldly curiosity, and it frees no one from the struggle of faith. This is true because Bethlehem is so much a part of our own world of darkness and poverty. No glory shines around the child's head, and no voices but our own speak God's word in the Holy Communion. No angel choirs can be heard here.

But please note that this is what "the Lord has made known to us." This shall be our sign: this child and this poverty, this bread and this wine. The word has said this, and says it again today. Let us go and see. Let us see that this is love. This is brotherhood. This is nearness. Isn't this what we were looking for? No God has made himself known save the one who loves in Bethlehem. God is love, and so it was that God loved the world. It is said elsewhere that those who have not seen, and yet believe, are blessed. This is said about everything we desire to help us to avoid believing, to help us to know and possess instead. But God's facts were given to us so that we should see and believe. As John said, "we have beheld his glory, glory as of the only Son from the Father," full of "grace and truth."

Our Brother Under the Stars

> *He was in the world, and the world was made
> through him, yet the world knew him not. He
> came to his own home, and his own people re-
> ceived him not.*
>
> —John 1:10–11

We are well acquainted with closed doors. Fear has closed
some, doubt has closed others. Each is closed for its own
reason. But this is not just the story of a divided community,
a broken friendship, a frayed marriage. "He came to his own
home, and his own people received him not." Was this not
also true of the man who came to the stones and trees and
the living dust? "Cursed is the ground because of you;/in toil
you shall eat of it all the days of your life;/thorns and thistles
it shall bring forth to you . . . ./In the sweat of your face/
you shall eat bread/till you return to the ground,/for out of it
you were taken;/you are dust,/and to dust you shall return."
Thus man became a stranger in the midst of what was once
his own. Finally, heaven was closed to him too, and he dwelt
in the cosmos as one unwelcome.

It was in this alien condition that Christ became one of
us; for he was one of us, born of a woman, placed under the
law and under the curse. But at the same time he was more
than this, for the world had been created through him. He
came to his own as to a work of art which had been created
out of his own thought and suffering. Yet he had to stand
outside of everything; all doors were closed to him; for him,

no room was to be found. He refused to be welcome without us, either in heaven or on earth. Heaven and earth must either receive sinners or exclude him; a choice had to be made. And to exclude him would be to erase the very signature of the one by whom the world came to be. There was a moment in which the world actually was for him, as well as for certain of us, without God and without hope.

Nevertheless, the atonement revealed its essence by permitting itself to be excluded, love revealed its essence by bearing the thorns as a crown. And not only its essence, such as it was from all eternity, such as it is to the very edge of all that can be known; he who is light of light has revealed the mystery in all that is. For it is, of course, his own, and it bears his stamp. Beyond enmity and the condition of being cursed, creation is a work of art shaped by love—pure love such as his. Because this is true, the crown of thorns which pricked his forehead is the crown of a king. He is king of the thorns, prince of the roses.

Now, as always, the bread we receive comes to us as a result of the efforts of others; their labor is included in the gift. And among all who serve to make such provisions is the Servant of servants. But when he came to his own, in pain and sorrow, the bread in his hand was no longer merely the fruit of a curse, for we saw his glory within it, "glory as of the only Son from the Father." The curse had been permeated by a blessing; so is the earth blessed when we live in his fellowship. O night of birth, when the cosmos burst and mysteries were revealed! In this Word, in this child, in this servant, in this bread the earth has become ours again, and welcomes us. The thorns are our mother, and they love us through this message whose secret the angels have desired to see.

The universe continues to lock its gates. Our hearts continue to shrink in the presence of death and dread. But when this becomes our only perspective, life becomes a snare in which mankind has already suffocated and which we in our anger pull all the tighter. This is our paramount sin: we believe in the darkness of the stall, but not in the mystery hidden there as in a jewel box. Let us confess our faithless fears and come to the Supper of the Lord. It is here that heaven is rent and earth redeemed, for he was in the world, and because of him the world is our home again. As happened one time at the dawn of creation, a great choir is singing in unison once again, the great choir of all that is — of earth and heaven, forests, clouds and mountains, seas and stars, angels, sparrows and roaring lions, the oak of our tables and the hearts in our breasts — they sing with us this night their *Gloria in Excelsis,* and gather around the child who is our brother, who is God of God, light of light.

The Ox and the Ass

> *"The ox knows its owner,*
> *and the ass its master's crib;*
> *but Israel does not know,*
> *my people does not understand."*
> —Isaiah 1:3

We have often seen the ox and the ass in the manger scene; Christian art continues to show them in the company of Mary and Joseph and the child, the shepherds and the wise men. They stand there in all of their animalistic simplicity; one has the impression that they will still be there after all of the others have gone.

But one could also say that they were there before all the others, not only before all artists and worshiping congregations, but before the shepherds and the wise men and Joseph and Mary. If they were there before the child is not easy to say. Sometimes it is easier to say where God is than to say where he is not, and the Bible says that the child in the manger existed before the manger and before the stall and before Bethlehem and before the world in which he rested.

But seven hundred years prior to the child's arrival Isaiah asserted that the ox and the ass know their "master's crib." Their behavior was something of a revelation, not because it was peculiar, but because it was so unreasoned, so unhesitating, so inevitable. A revelation of what it is to be at home, to know one's way, to be faithful. "But Israel does not know,/ my people does not understand." The prophet testified in vain to the fact that his people, a self-assured, enlightened, and progressive nation, were rushing pell-mell toward destruction, eyes wide open, while the voice of God cried after them, unheard. Bitterly the prophet pointed to the ox and ass as a model for this people: "The ox knows its owner,/and the ass its master's crib."

And there they are now, every time a crèche is built and children sing

> When Christmas morn is dawning
>   In faith I would repair
> Unto the lowly manger;
>   My Saviour lieth there.

They are there not as a legendary embellishment of the gospel but as a reminder of the fact that the event reflects reality. Many believe that Christmas is just a fairy tale, with teddy bears and Santa Claus bearing his sack of trains and dolls and other toys — and then, too, the baby Jesus. Great crowds of sensible people stand outside the display windows, drawn to the never-never land within, not only by their insistent children, but by the pent-up desire to play, to become as children again in a land where all wishes are wonderfully fulfilled and where people play at peace on earth. But soon they revert to what they consider real life. War, in great issues and in small. Jealousy and slander. Love that is a lie, and hate that is the truth. Days without contentment and without prayer. Realities. This is humanity, this is America, this is Sweden, this is our town, we believe, shorn of its Christmas glitter and its fresh blanket of snow.

But the ox and the ass are faithful. When toyland has ceased to be, and the Christmas tree has been shorn of its last bauble, and men have returned to their customary occupations, the ox will still know his master, and the ass his crib. From Christmas to Christmas they continue to bear mute testimony under yoke and saddle, their hooves stamping mysterious symbols in the dust, an evangelical cipher code on the way to and from the stall, a message concerning service which our Savior himself verified when he took a stall for his dwelling place.

And if mankind could read, it would know and understand that heaven and earth, angels and animals, the stars in the sky and marks of grief — each confirms the gospel of Luke, certifying that this is our home, this is where we belong. All the rest, the so-called realities, are a dreadful fabrication, an all-inclusive dementia, real enough as systematic madness and seduction, but an alien reality; we didn't come from this and we won't return thence — that is not where we live. Not in the Christmas industry, not in this great restlessness, but with the little one who is God's peace. The gospel is not a game, is is not a dream, it is a serious message from God, from home.

But do we take it seriously? We complain about the lack of peace in the world and about the meaninglessness of our existence, but it is we who lack peace, and it is we who use the world in meaningless ways. But peace can be found, and meaning too, for the gospel has become an earthly reality, to be believed and practiced. To live in. And this is to return home. But it has been so long since man departed from home that a message from God is treated as a game, a sparkling toy, a decorative transparency. Christmas follows Christmas, but as God's word says, "Israel does not know,/my people does not understand."

Thus it was that the prophet, with heaven's characteristically mild irony, permitted the ass to lecture those who have understanding, and the ox those who learn with ease. According to Numbers, Balaam journeyed forth as though there were no angels, and his ass rescued him from a dangerous collision with a bit of reality from heaven. The ass, you see, understood such things better than the restless prophet. That was neither the first nor the last time that a man has been rebuked by such an envoy.

The ox and the ass also provide the correct answer to the question about empty churches, since Bethlehem's stall is no less significant for man just because most people were asleep at the time when the shepherds came. Their report was the first Christmas sermon; we are not told that the ox and the ass understood it, but they were there. The angels provided the choir for this first Christmas service; we are not told that the ox and the ass appreciated music, but they were there, for "the ox knows its owner,/and the ass its master's crib." What holy humor, to hide this from the wise and knowing, but to reveal it to the simple!

So it was in the beginning, when the wellspring of wisdom appeared in man. So it continued, in the obedience of Christmas, in everyday agony, in the suffering of St. Stephen's day. Many were willing, provided that they could be sure it was worthwhile. But the ox and the ass did not ask for guarantees; they were simply there. No wonder that the ox is the symbol of Luke the Evangelist, and that the only creature the Lord needed (as far as we are told) was an ass and her colt.

But if the ox and ass thus put the wisdom of the world to shame that holy night, so are they also of great solace to shepherds and other simple country folks who are frightened of angels but who feel at home with animals. Do not forget the ox and the ass, all you who feel excluded from the most holy, excluded because you are sinners and ignorant and ordinary and profane. Not everyone has a star to follow, as did the three kings. The rest of us must do as the shepherds did, and follow the animals to the stall where God's peace has taken his dwelling place. For "the ox knows its owner,/ and the ass its master's crib." Thank God for them.

Commitment

> *"Therefore I send you prophets and wise men and scribes, some of whom you will kill and crucify, and some you will scourge in your synagogues and persecute from town to town, that upon you may come all the righteous blood shed on earth, from the blood of innocent Abel to the blood of Zechariah the son of Barachiah, whom you murdered between the sanctuary and the altar. Truly, I say to you, all this will come upon this generation.*
>
> *"O Jerusalem, Jerusalem, killing the prophets and stoning those who are sent to you! How often would I have gathered your children together as a hen gathers her brood under her wings, and you would not! Behold, your house is forsaken and desolate. For I tell you, you will not see me again, until you say, 'Blessed is he who comes in the name of the Lord.'"*
>
> —Matthew 23:34–39

God has involved himself in the life of this world, not only as a creative power, but as one of us. It is written that he came in the form of a servant. We learn at Christmas about the time and circumstances in which this encounter took place. Augustus was the Roman Emperor at the time, Quirinius was the governor of Syria — and a Jewish family of royal lineage served as the gateway through which God entered into history. We are not surprised to hear that the family so honored was chosen from within a holy nation, but it is remarkable that this happened in such miserable and obscure circumstances.

Today we have come to see that this encounter has been planned. "Therefore I send you prophets and wise men and scribes . . . ." Luke tells us in his Gospel that these words were taken from the "wisdom of God," which is to say that they do not simply constitute a rejoinder in Jesus' debate with his countrymen. Rather, they summarize a divine plan for the ages. This same plan is also interpreted in the first chapter of Hebrews, an ancient Christmas text, where we read that God has spoken to us through his son, after having spoken "in many and various ways . . . to our fathers by the prophets." This is the spiritual tradition in which the Christmas gospel has its place.

If one uses the word "tradition" in this connection, one must never forget that the envoys referred to frequently called into question the traditional patterns of thought. It was part and parcel of the prophetic tradition to be unfettered by custom. Not because it represented that which was current and modern; the prophets spoke directly to the social and political situation — they were by all means *au courant*. But they represented conventional thinking as little as they were borne up by the opinions of the day. They were sure that they had been sent to proclaim justice, mercy, and faithfulness in direct opposition to both customary and fashionable trends of thought. What this implied can be seen in the first chapter of Jeremiah, where the voice of God speaks thus: "And I, behold, I make you this day a fortified city, an iron pillar, and bronze walls, against the whole land, against the kings of Judah, its princes, its priests, and the people of the land."

The fact that God involved himself in the history of the world does not depend therefore upon certain romantic illusions concerning the nature of the world. The wisdom of God realizes that the prophetic tradition is a tradition of martyrdoms, all the way from Genesis and the righteous Abel to the second book of Chronicles (the last book in the Jewish Bible) and the priest Zechariah, who was murdered between the temple and the altar. When God committed himself most fully, without any reservations, he took the risk of being treated just as the prophets were. This also provides us with the key to the unusually harsh notes in the Christmas gospel that bear witness to reservations about God's having become man. The cross is included.

The strange part of all this is that the prophets were killed by a chosen people — referred to as God's own — and that this was done in their capital, which was called the holy city. It was these people who preserved the writings of the prophets and instructed generation after generation in their teachings. While Jesus lived men said, "If we had lived in the days of our fathers, we would not have taken part with them in shedding the blood of the prophets." But that same generation crucified Jesus and stoned Stephen.

In the New Testament, one can detect enormous indignation over the fact that the Jews of the upper echelons closed their eyes to the gospel and locked their doors against the early church. The Christians must have come close to saying, "We will not take part with them," and to thinking of themselves as the new people of God — the heirs of the prophets. There were also situations in which the words of the Sermon on the Mount could be applied to the early Christians: "for so men persecuted the prophets who were before you." But alongside these texts we find expressions of disappointment, not with the Jews, but with Christians. The Book of Revelation says this about an entire congregation: "you have the name of being alive, and you are dead." To this the author adds, "Yet you have still a few names in Sardis, people who have not soiled their garments." This is a familiar situation: a religious community within which there are individuals who do not submit to discipline because they heed a message from another source. The texts which tell us about faithless Israel, and about Jerusalem that killed the prophets, have with the passing of time been applied in other ways too. They no longer refer exclusively to the Jews. The reckoning accorded the old Israel provided basic textual material for reckoning with the new Israel, the church. For just as the old Israel preserved the words of the prophets but forgot to apply them, so does the new Jerusalem administer the gospel, forgetting all too often to apply it. Thus it is that the cross is raised anew in the Christian world.

The hardest part of being a martyr is probably not the physical pain, but the loneliness. We all seek the approval of our fellowmen when we set forth our opinions. With strong support we can dare to do many things. But the message of the martyrs was often unpopular, and many of them were forced to speak out in direct opposition to public opinion. It is not our task today to make amends to them in some way, as people in Jesus' time built sepulchers for the prophets, but rather to heed the message which they sealed.

If we seek that message in our text, we find first of all a surprisingly mild and seemingly innocuous parable. Christ reminds us here of the fact that the female bird (not just the hen, as it says in the translation), gathers her young under her wings. So had he often wanted to place the people who lived in Jerusalem under his protection. But Jerusalem had not wanted such protection. Many of the prophets had come to the defense of those unjustly treated, the homeless, the poorly paid, the immigrants. They recognized that the welfare of the entire nation depended, in the final analysis, upon the manner in which such problems were solved. With Christ's coming, divine love itself came to the defense of the defenseless — and of the entire nation. This was no longer a proclamation inspired by a God in the clouds and the mist. This was a presence. The maternal image of the female bird protecting her young is a picture of God's presence in the world; and this ceases to be a meaningless and innocuous picture as soon as we glimpse the shadow of the vulture gliding, cross-shaped, over the field.

This gospel, which the church has so often denied, nevertheless now confronts us. A murmur of voices — from prophets, apostles, martyrs — crying, warning, comforting, will prompt us at some time to challenge the assumptions which surround us — secular assumptions as well as pious assumptions. Even ecclesiastical assumptions. To be attuned to this depth of responsibility, of mercy, of suffering, is to be attuned to God's own essence. To return to the world — the world of piety and impiety — after such an experience is to return with a profound insight concerning both the world and the God who loved it so. This is to return with sensitive ears. To have such an experience and then to be deaf to need — to the need reflected in pictures of war, in statistics of abortion, in the need of new nations, in the journals of mental hospitals, in the wordless appeal of a fellow human being who chances to cross our path — to be deaf to such need is to crucify God in one's heart. In the gospel, social responsibility and the thirst for eternal life speak the same language, for the source is the same: the God who so loved the world.

A significant result of this is pointed to at the end of our text: to be called into God's involvement with the world is to be called out to the precipice where history plunges headlong into eternity. It may seem tempting to hide oneself in the opinions of the day, or perhaps in a religious gathering or observance, where the winds from the immediately surrounding areas envelop us. To look upon the world as an eternal reality, to find eternity entangled in pious or impious secularity — both of these possibilities seem frightening for those who, with Stephen, have studied the results of what happened in Bethlehem. They will remember perhaps an apostolic admonition to use the prophets as an example in enduring tribulation, and to be prepared for the worst.

Nevertheless, it is not moaning and groaning which we find in this part of the gospel. It is heaven opened up over Stephen's martyrdom. Listen, too, to that passage in our text where we are confronted with the ultimate realities.

Hunger cries out here too, need reaches out for fulfillment, and this is expressed in an ancient song from Jerusalem, a song that echoes through the centuries, down to the last tribulation, in the thanksgiving of the Lord's Supper: "*Blessed* is he who comes in the name of the Lord!"

The Cry of Ramah

Now when they had departed, behold, an angel of the Lord appeared to Joseph in a dream and said, "Rise, take the child and his mother, and flee to Egypt, and remain there till I tell you; for Herod is about to search for the child, to destroy him." And he rose and took the child and his mother by night, and departed to Egypt, and remained there until the death of Herod. This was to fulfil what the Lord had spoken by the prophet, "Out of Egypt have I called my son."

Then Herod, when he saw that he had been tricked by the wise men, was in a furious rage, and he sent and killed all the male children in Bethlehem and in all that region who were two years old or under, according to the time which he had ascertained from the wise men. Then was fulfilled what was spoken by the prophet Jeremiah:

> *"A voice was heard in Ramah,*
> *wailing and loud lamentation,*
> *Rachel weeping for her children;*
> *she refused to be consoled,*
> *because they were no more."*

But when Herod died, behold, an angel of the Lord appeared in a dream to Joseph in Egypt, saying, "Rise, take the child and his mother, and go to the land of Israel, for those who sought the child's life are dead." And he rose and took the child and his mother, and went to the land of Israel. But when he heard that Archelaus reigned over Judea in place of his father Herod, he was afraid to go there, and being warned in a dream he

> *withdrew to the district of Galilee. And he went*
> *and dwelt in a city called Nazareth, that what was*
> *spoken by the prophets might be fulfilled, "He*
> *shall be called a Nazarene."*
>
> —Matthew 2:13–23

"Rise, take the child and his mother, and flee . . . ." Thus it is that the stillness of Christmas is broken; when we read this we get the impression that Christmas itself is torn asunder. Not even the holy family escaped this disturbance of Christmas. Mary woke the child in the night, prepared him for a long journey, took him in her arms, hoping that he would not cry — not then, and above all not later, when they would cross the border. Farewell, Bethlehem — probably the child noticed the anxious look on Mary's face, the haste of her movements, the tension in her hands, but, "Don't cry," she said.

The landscape over which they traveled is the familiar territory of the Bible. Not far from Bethlehem is the grave of Rachel, beloved of the patriarch Jacob, who died there along the road after giving birth to her son Benjamin (or *Ben–Oni,* "son of my suffering"). Many centuries later, the nucleus of the tribe of Benjamin was deported far to the east, and when the prophet Jeremiah looked back upon this event he thought he could hear the groaning of Rachel over the entire area, from the soil in which she was buried: "A voice is heard in Ramah, lamentation and bitter weeping." And the Evangelist who stood and watched the refugees could hear how the darkness over the land of Benjamin continued to tremble with the weeping of Rachel. He knew what was to happen.

The church has reported this for nineteen centuries. She has engraved this passage from Matthew's Gospel upon time, as upon an endless band. It is the Gospel for the Feast of the Holy Innocents. This story has not been repeated year after

year in order to bring the judgment of history down upon
Herod, as though it had been only during his regime that
children were put to death. Rather, the text has served as a
mirror in which every age can recognize itself. For even
though methods and motives change, generation after generation and society after society have seen to it that unwelcome
children are shunted aside — or done away with. History,
B. C. and A. D., is filled with Rachel's sorrow.

The road of the refugees also runs through time and space.
The Evangelist read further in his biblical geography. There
are Jacob and his sons, running from hunger to the granaries
of Egypt. Four hundred years later the Israelites returned,
fleeing Pharaoh and his army. Hosea the prophet celebrated
this miraculous deliverance with words of divine mercy:
"When Israel was a child, I loved him, and out of Egypt I
called my son." But the same Evangelist who quotes these
words also reports that Jesus, in referring to the end of time
and the great tribulation, gave special thought to refugees,
and particularly to the mothers and children among them:
"And alas for those who are with child and for those who
give suck in those days! Pray that your flight may not be in
winter or on a sabbath." However far the road of refugees
stretches, the caravans remain long, with groups and individuals fleeing their Pharaohs, their Herods, or nameless
hunger, a city on fire or an invading sea. And mothers and
children are never lacking among them.

So the gospel takes into consideration all of this that we
have in mind when we ask if there can be a God of love.
These questions are not smoothed over in the Bible; as a matter of fact, these red letters hit us in the eye all the way from
Genesis to Revelation. There it is that our questions to God
become God's questions to us; God wants to know how we
can permit such things as the slaughter of the innocents in
Bethlehem. And God's question comes, not from the throne

of majesty, but from one of the refugees: "Truly, I say to you, as you did it to one of the least of these my brethren, you did it to me."

God has not put the blame on someone else, as though he wanted to participate in a debate with an atheist; his word comes from Bethlehem, from the child in Mary's arms, from the day of the Holy Innocents. It is from there that God speaks to us. He himself became one of these children. Yes, his own life is a map on which all men can find their Ramah, and all refugees their way through the wilderness. An abstract of the landscape of suffering can be found here.

But there is also a king's residence on this landscape — an alternative to Herod's Jerusalem. In the name of the hiding place where this flight finally ended Matthew perceives the fulfillment of a promise made long before. According to that promise, a branch should grow up out of the root of Jesse; and the letters of the Hebrew word for "branch" are also found in the name of the town where the holy family came to reside: Nazareth. This Branch of David's house, this king of the Jews, was the one whom the astrologers from the East came to worship. See how he wears his crown. "He shall be called a Nazarene." He shall be called a refugee. He shall be called powerless. And, at the last, Mary shall stand and see them put to death her child, the son of her sorrow, and Rachel's lamentation shall surge through her like a racking pain. Then it was that a superscription was placed over his dying form, in Latin, in Greek — but also in Hebrew. It said: "Jesus of Nazareth, king of the Jews." But those who were well versed in the Scriptures knew that this also said, "Jesus the Branch, king of the Jews." That which was intended to be mockery was seen by some as a fulfillment. What was fulfilled? The true kingdom. God with us.

"He shall be called a Nazarene." What do we call him?

It is obvious that we must choose between two ways of

writing history. As seen from Herod's point of view, the day of the Innocents is an insignificant detail. A friend of Herod's wrote the history of his reign, and in it this event is not even mentioned. It was not considered necessary to defend Herod for such an unimportant matter. Other historians have recorded many gruesome episodes from his career, events similar to this one but of greater consequence to Jerusalem or Rome.

The other way of writing history originates in Nazareth. A child is king there. A refugee. One who has been executed. There it is that history fuses together the old and the new, prophecy and the daily news. Piercing all that is set forth as important because some politician has said so, or all men, or the daily papers, or TV — piercing all of this, the Evangelist wants to bring us to ask who is right, Herod or Jesus. To ask if this is one of these greatest or one of these least in determining what is important. To ask if power or mercy is to have the last word.

This question is not raised merely for purposes of examination. Each of us possesses a place of refuge beyond and below all Herodian officialdom. Nazareth is here, in the gospel and at the altar. We are baptized into that. As children we were included in the gospel; our history was incorporated into that of the Nazarene. In his community the history of Jesus Christ and these little ones is actually present. This is summarized in the confession of sin and the absolution, in worship and the breaking of the bread. Here, anew, the life of the defenseless man becomes Christ's own life, and his life becomes the defenseless man's. Who is the defenseless man? He who knows no other place of refuge. He who finds himself without assistance when it really matters — without the assistance of the power and influence of Herod the Great or any other lord. Child and sinner, at wit's end.

He who seeks for the child in order to find the answer to his question and help in time of need discovers the way back to Christmas. The Gospel for the Feast of the Holy Innocents takes its place, ultimately, not outside the Christmas gospel, but in its very heart. Christmas decorations and Christmas festivities lie farther on; those who come there find out that they have made a mistake — as though the wise men had remained at Herod's palace. But God is with us, with Rachel in Ramah and with Mary in Nazareth, for the child is there, the child who is God's love to these least.

It is there too that the road leads out of Egypt, out of Herod's land and time, out of the shadow of death to that future and that hope which belongs to Jesus of Nazareth and the innocent children, saints and sinners in his kingdom. The prophet Jeremiah spoke about this in the continuation of the passage quoted above: "Thus says the Lord:/'Keep your voice from weeping,/and your eyes from tears; . . ./There is hope for your future,/says the Lord,/and your children shall come back to their own country.' "

Which country? The country in which we are properly at home. "God himself will be with them," it says of the people there; "he will wipe away every tear from their eyes, and death shall be no more, neither shall there be mourning nor crying nor pain any more, for the former things have passed away."

III

Let Him Who
Is Thirsty Come

Decision

And when he was twelve years old, they went up according to custom; and when the feast was ended, as they were returning, the boy Jesus stayed behind in Jerusalem. His parents did not know it, but supposing him to be in the company they went a day's journey, and they sought him among their kinsfolk and acquaintances; and when they did not find him, they returned to Jerusalem, seeking him. After three days they found him in the temple, sitting among the teachers, listening to them and asking them questions; and all who heard him were amazed at his understanding and his answers. And when they saw him they were astonished; and his mother said to him, "Son, why have you treated us so? Behold, your father and I have been looking for you anxiously." And he said to them, "How is it that you sought me? Did you not know that I must be in my Father's house?" And they did not understand the saying which he spoke to them. And he went down with them and came to Nazareth, and was obedient to them; and his mother kept all these things in her heart.

And Jesus increased in wisdom and in stature, and in favor with God and man.

—Luke 2:42–52

We have become accustomed to look upon this text as a picture in which a pale and delicate boy surprises his teachers with his insight into religious questions. The setting is in a church, which strengthens the impression that this is an unusually good and innocent child.

But take note of several details in the text.

First, that the twelve-year-old's decision to remain behind in the temple is understood as a challenge to his parents. The author was obliged to establish, for safety's sake, that upon returning home, and in the future, the youth was loyal to them. Additional cases of insubordination are not mentioned. But this event is the first in a series of conflicts, as a dreadful mission wrenched Jesus of Nazareth away from home and relatives and friends. The last conflict is reported at another Passover, when the nation's highest authority condemned him to death.

At the same time, however, this was a mission which led into a deeper loyalty toward nation and people. It is not surprising that a twelve-year-old stayed behind too long in this center of his people's destiny, with all of its historic memories. But the report of this is peculiarly agitated. We get the impression of questions presented under great tension, as though the young man had begun to sense a fateful hidden meaning in what he saw there. The record indicates that he was not merely pleased to be visiting the temple: "I must be in my Father's house." Or more properly: "I ought to be in that which is my Father's." This is a question, not just of a sacred building, but of a sacred dimension. Thus it was that he entered into his people's memory: with a fateful son-consciousness. Fateful — for being God's son signified a messianic identification with God's son among the people, with Israel. We also see, time after time, events in his life in which he, so to speak, recapitulates the fortunes of his people. The flight to Egypt, for example: "Out of Egypt have I called my son." Also the forty days in the desert, corresponding to the forty years of wandering in the wilderness. And his baptism in the Jordan, that important boundary river. Subsequent to that, his journeys into the actual needs of the people on the public roads. Finally, his suffering and death, which incarnated the prophetic songs of a people who were God's servants, bearing the curse of the world.

He sat among the teachers, "listening to them and asking them questions." This was a striking kind of boldness; twelve-year-old boys do not associate in this way with professors. But we are not speaking here of a gifted Sunday school pupil; we are confronted here by a relentless seeking.

Without resisting, he was taken to the border country where a discovery was being prepared, where an inquiring begins which can easily be disposed of, but which cannot really be silenced or stopped. Might it be that the mother's reprimand expressed her intuitive insight into what was coming? If she had really understood what was beginning here, she ought to have cried, "Don't ask, child, don't ask any more!" For the time was coming when she would return home from the festival alone.

This seeking was completely genuine. Jesus the Messiah received nothing gratis; he had to ask and seek. He did not bypass the authorities. One of his truly human qualities can be seen in the fact that he was subordinate, not only to the humble folk of Galilee, but also to the theologians who would one day actively contribute to his death. But when this seeker appeared before the authorities to ask and ask, he knew nothing of church politics or theological schools, nothing of professorships, nor of anything which peeks around corners and sniffs to right and left. When this guileless young man stood there and asked his questions, all that this world calls authority trembled. The translations which tell us that all who heard him were "amazed" are extremely cautious, for the key word in the text hints at a situation in which men were beside themselves, not knowing which way to turn.

Thus it was that the judgment of him who is the brother of all seekers can already be discerned in this unusual temple incident. But when we read this it is not easy to remain uninvolved. There is the danger that this text is not simply an account of how he went deeper into his own destiny, but that it poses a question to us who read it, a question concerning our destiny. How much do we dare to ask, how much do we dare to seek — and do we dare do this with him, together with him? Some might thus discover their own calling, and as a result might find no way out of the history of Jesus Christ on earth.

Wine and the Jars of Purification

> On the third day there was a marriage at Cana in
> Galilee, and the mother of Jesus was there; Jesus
> also was invited to the marriage, with his disciples.
> When the wine failed, the mother of Jesus said to
> him, "They have no wine." And Jesus said to her,
> "O woman, what have you to do with me? My
> hour has not yet come." His mother said to the
> servants, "Do whatever he tells you." Now six
> stone jars were standing there, for the Jewish rites
> of purification, each holding twenty or thirty gal-
> lons. Jesus said to them, "Fill the jars with water."
> And they filled them up to the brim. He said to
> them, "Now draw some out, and take it to the
> steward of the feast." So they took it. When the
> steward of the feast tasted the water now become
> wine, and did not know where it came from
> (though the servants who had drawn the water
> knew), the steward of the feast called the bride-
> groom and said to him, "Every man serves the good
> wine first; and when men have drunk freely, then
> the poor wine; but you have kept the good wine
> until now." This, the first of his signs, Jesus did at
> Cana in Galilee, and manifested his glory; and his
> disciples believed in him.
>
> —John 2:1–11

"They have no wine" — a housewife's concern, but Christ
did not despise it. The entire celebration was at stake, really,
for how would it go with a wedding in Cana if the wine ran
out? For years to come it would be said about this bridal pair

that it was at their wedding that the wine failed. At this moment, no question was more important in this little world, in Cana, in a housewife's heart. And no world is too little and no concern too humble for Christ, not even a kitchen and a worry about having enough wine.

Was it only in Cana that Christ tarried until his hour had come? Was it only there and then that the wine began to run out and the servants filled the jars of purification to the brim — though not with wine? Was it only those cups which were filled with the good wine, the kind that had been long lacking and long anticipated? Was it only then when Christ revealed his glory?

If one lingers a moment with this passage, looking into it as a man might gaze down into a well, a picture of a larger cosmos can be discerned on the quivering surface. Not another reality, but the very essence of time compressed into a few moments before the hour had come. The essence of time when the wine began to run short; when the wedding lost its lustre and people tried to cover up the lack behind gales of laughter; when perplexity ran from room to room, busy without rhyme or reason; when all our love and all of our longing burst into a commonplace phrase, a farsighted disappointment: they have no wine.

What good are the jars of purification to us? The long line of servants who taught us rites and rules? The wisdom of the Greeks and the ablutions of the Jews? When the measure is full, clarity has been achieved — the clarity to see that no water could purify our love and make us worthy of the festival of life. It is there that our worship begins. It begins with that which remains after all has been washed in the confession of sin — a factual account of the situation as it is in a world of longing without fulfillment and of purification without joy. And our cups are empty.

But he was among us, not only in Cana; he shared our joy,

and was well acquainted with our needs. But he remained among us until his hour had come. Then the mystery involved in the wedding at Cana was made clear. Then all of the prophecies concerning purification were fulfilled. Then the festival wore white robes and our cups overflowed. This chalice is the new testament. So it was that he revealed his glory — when his hour had come, and love was fulfilled in suffering. This was the first sign that Jesus did; he did it in Cana of Galilee, he did it on the night when he was betrayed, he does it here and now, for his disciples were invited to the wedding too — and such are we, we who know that we must be where he is. To whom should we go?

You see, this is our festival. This is our life. To love. To devote ourselves to the purification of all that has been vain. In this his cup is lifted, and his word proclaimed from the night of suffering. And the wine shall not fail. This concerns our life and our longing, our love and all our vain ritual. See the candle which is lit for the festival — in it his joy and his suffering, everything is enclosed.

Enclosed in a sign, and we saw its mystery. We saw that all has been fulfilled. But it was fulfilled in a sign, and there it was that we saw his glory, enclosed in the sign provided by the wine, as under a seal. John reports this as one who is saying something in a way that also tells us something more.

The time is coming when the seal will be broken, and we shall see what kind of festival we are involved in. Then shall the banal jest of the restaurateur burst, and a hymn of love rise from it: "you have kept the good wine until now." Then his promise about the fruit of the vine — that he will drink it anew in his Father's kingdom — shall be fulfilled. Then shall our Cana lie in the holy land.

This is our Cana, and this is our festival. This is our life. So it is that the mysterious sign is present, and the cup of blessing blessed. It is written in the Book of Revelation: "The Spirit and the Bride say, 'Come.' And let him who hears say, 'Come.' And let him who is thirsty come, let him who desires take the water of life without price."

If Any One Thirst

How lovely is thy dwelling place,
   O Lord of hosts!
My soul longs, yea, faints
   for the courts of the Lord;
my heart and flesh sing for joy
   to the living God.

Even the sparrow finds a home,
   and the swallow a nest for herself,
   where she may lay her young,
at thy altars, O Lord of hosts,
   my King and my God.
Blessed are those who dwell in thy house,
   ever singing thy praise!

Blessed are the men whose strength is in thee,
   in whose heart are the highways to Zion.
As they go through the valley of Baca
   they make it a place of springs;
   the early rain also covers it with pools.
They go from strength to strength;
   the God of gods will be seen in Zion.

O Lord God of hosts, hear my prayer;
   give ear, O God of Jacob!
Behold our shield, O God;
   look upon the face of thine anointed!

For a day in thy courts is better
   than a thousand elsewhere.
I would rather be a doorkeeper in the house of my God
   than dwell in the tents of wickedness.
For the Lord God is a sun and shield;
   he bestows favor and honor.

*No good thing does the Lord withhold
  from those who walk uprightly.
O Lord of hosts,
  blessed is the man who trusts in thee!*

—Psalm 84

"Look upon the face of thine anointed!" This refers to the king, as he nears the temple in festal procession. Pilgrims surround him, and their presence calls down a blessing upon the land; when they return, it rains over the dry valleys, as though water from the spring at Siloam, mixed with wine and poured out at the altar, flooded over the thirsty earth.

This longing is not only felt by the earth. The king sees the swallows that build nests in the walls of the forecourt and now and then dart down over the altar of sacrifice. Men do not always have homes for themselves and their children; even the king of Israel learned to know grief. Not only in battle and in danger. Sometimes it is easier to feel at home in a tent than in a palace. But one day in the courts of the Lord — "my heart and flesh sing for joy." Like the birds and the Levites, so would the king also desire to dwell close to the altar, there to praise God without ceasing. The Hebrew expression "jehalluka" rings with the sound of jubilee.

But the answer comes to king and people from the sons of Korah, the great Levitical choir, who sing of the man whose strength is in God, the man of blessing who calls down rain from heaven and makes the springs flow in the dry valleys, and who helps the king to pray: God, "look upon the face of thine anointed."

Here the Bible reader stops during the first week after the Epiphany, and observes that the basic text tells us "to look upon the face of the Messiah."

Jesus too was familiar with these words; perhaps he joined in the song about the joys of the temple when, at the age of twelve, he first visited there. He already knew something about that which he later described in a picture which is reminiscent of the sparrows and swallows in our text: "Foxes have holes, and birds of the air have nests; but the Son of man has nowhere to lay his head." The road already inclined toward solitude; he had already left behind him the one home he could ever call his own. His mission loomed before him, steeper than the road up Zion hill. The world, more desolate than the wilds of Judah, awaited its Messiah. But the ancient prayers and rites and symbols of the temple gave answer to the cry of his heart, and when Mary finally found him there, her uncomprehending question provided confirmation: here was where he, like the swallows in the temple walls, really belonged; he was already homeless in Nazareth.

But twenty years later, at the very feast celebrated in this psalm, he stood there and cried out about springs and the autumn rain: "If any one thirst, let him come to me and drink." Like other devout men, he knew what it means to say that the heart dwells at the altar. It means that one can always recapture a sense of calm there. It means that one's thoughts can be collected there, like carrier pigeons, as soon as the work and worry of the day fold their wings. It means that one can hear the sacred springs far beneath the chatter and plans and decisions of the day, even though one finds himself lonely miles from the altar. "If any one thirst, let him come to *me* . . . ."

The temple too was shut closed to him. The twelve-year-old's troubled and dangerous questions were finally answered by the priests and the scribes. He got the same answers as the sinners, the heathens, and the Samaritans. And what answer did God give? "Behold our shield, O God;/look upon the face of thine anointed." A prayer for all who found their Messiah in him. A prayer for needy lands and anxious souls. What kind of answer was that? He asked that himself. And that question can be found in another royal psalm: "My God, my God, why hast thou forsaken me?" For the Psalter provided this prince of all wretched sinners not only with answers, but also with questions. We are also told of the twelve-year-old in the temple that he confronted the scribes, "asking them questions."

The Lord does not reject those who walk uprightly." But what of those who dwell in the tents of wickedness? Those who do not qualify to receive the blessing of the temple?

He became our Christ. He wants no answer from the temple other than the one intended for us.

Loneliness prevails when the temple is not a home. There is a restlessness like that of the swallow whose nest has been destroyed and whose young have been cast out: she swoops in wide circles around the devastation, uttering shrill cries. The soul returns to the temple one day, but it finds neither a fortress nor a dwelling place. Peace is gone. The blessing is dead. Heaven is closed. The soil is parched.

"If any one thirst . . . ." Jesus the Messiah said that. In the final analysis, he is the only answer. The temple is in ruins, but his voice continues to speak. God has hidden his face, but Jesus the Messiah has turned his face toward us. Yes, God has looked upon his Messiah. The "glory which shines forth" in his face is God's answer. That is why he, at the end, received no answer. That is why he never had a home. He himself became our home, with God.

For this reason, the church is a place of refuge. The essence of the church is not to be found in tranquility, in pomp and ceremony, in the strength of its stone walls, or in the beauty of song. But in the gospel of Jesus Christ. The banquet of reconciliation for those who hunger and thirst. Priests and scribes, choirs and congregations, festivals and daily quarrels — all of this changes, and one day will be gone, without one stone left upon the other. But where he is, there the swallow has a nest. Let the homeless overcome his anxiety and draw near. Standing before closed doors and ruined temples, the heart feels strong doubts — like the frightened bird defending itself from those who try to help. But come to the outstretched hand: "If any one thirst, let him come to me." He speaks the truth; you can take him at his word, which springs from the hard reality that is ours, his and ours.

For his sake, and in his name, springs of living water can also be found in this world. The seared life, the parched soul — this is the soil from which his blessing is to break forth. "If any one thirst, let him come to me and drink. He who believes in me, . . . 'Out of his heart shall flow rivers of living water.' "

The Well

So he came to a city of Samaria, called Sychar,
near the field that Jacob gave to his son Joseph.
Jacob's well was there, and so Jesus, wearied as he
was with his journey, sat down beside the well. It
was about the sixth hour.

There came a woman of Samaria to draw water.
Jesus said to her, "Give me a drink." For his disciples had gone away into the city to buy food.
The Samaritan woman said to him, "How is it
that you, a Jew, ask a drink of me, a woman of
Samaria?" For Jews have no dealings with Samaritans. Jesus answered her, "If you knew the gift of
God, and who it is that is saying to you, 'Give me
a drink,' you would have asked him, and he would
have given you living water." The woman said to
him, "Sir, you have nothing to draw with, and the
well is deep; where do you get that living water?
Are you greater than our father Jacob, who gave
us the well, and drank from it himself, and his
sons, and his cattle?" Jesus said to her, "Every one
who drinks of this water will thirst again, but whoever drinks of the water that I shall give him will
never thirst; the water that I shall give him will become in him a spring of water welling up to eternal
life." The woman said to him, "Sir, give me this
water, that I may not thirst, nor come here to
draw."

Jesus said to her, "Go, call your husband, and
come here." The woman answered him, "I have no
husband." Jesus said to her, "You are right in saying, 'I have no husband'; for you have had five
husbands, and he whom you now have is not your

> husband; this you said truly." The woman said to
> him, "Sir, I perceive that you are a prophet. Our
> fathers worshiped on this mountain; and you say
> that in Jerusalem is the place where men ought to
> worship." Jesus said to her, "Woman, believe me,
> the hour is coming when neither on this mountain
> nor in Jerusalem will you worship the Father. You
> worship what you do not know; we worship what
> we know, for salvation is from the Jews. But the
> hour is coming, and now is, when the true wor-
> shipers will worship the Father in spirit and truth,
> for such the Father seeks to worship him. God is
> spirit, and those who worship him must worship in
> spirit and truth." The woman said to him, "I know
> that Messiah is coming (he who is called Christ);
> when he comes, he will show us all things." Jesus
> said to her, "I who speak to you am he."
>
> —John 4:5–26

Men have speculated a great deal about the woman at the
well of Sychar in Samaria to whom, in the stifling heat of
midday, Christ spoke about the living water. There are inter-
preters who say that the account doesn't deal with a woman
at all, but with the Samaritan religion. Properly speaking, it is
said, this was a theological discussion involving the Samaritan
religion, Judaism, and Christianity; and the woman at the
well served as an allegorical figure, or, perhaps, merely as a
figure in the landscape.

As a rule, however, the Johannine texts have more than one
dimension. And even though a religious discussion can be
discerned in the background this text retains its quality of
personal soul care. Even if the woman does serve as an
allegorical figure, the fact that she is depicted in such a vital,
personal way is all the more important. Furthermore, it is
impossible for those who know something about thirsting for
God to read this text without recognizing themselves. We can
be sure that the Evangelist knew this too.

It frequently happens in the Bible that the destiny of an individual serves to gather up and symbolize the situation of a nation, of humanity, and in the final analysis of the entire creation.

Sermons based on this text have often dealt, in part at least, with this woman's morals. Why did she come to the well at this time of the day unless she was trying to avoid meeting anyone? And when Jesus led the conversation into a consideration of thirst, we may wonder if this was not a word that went directly into the situation of this woman who had gone from man to man and who at this time was living with a man who was not her husband. This great concern for a soul driven to search for something, and not least of all to an endless erotic search seems extremely modern.

But nothing says that she who is called the Samaritan woman had been driven out of one relationship and into another by any kind of a thirst save the one that on this day had brought her out into the blazing sunshine. At that time and in that place, where should a divorced woman go to find — I will not say love, but food to eat and a roof over her head, if not to another man? As long as the man, in turn, found it desirable to keep her. No matter what it was that contributed to her five divorces and the humiliating and conscience-searing situation she now lived in, it was not difficult to understand — above all at the well there in that sun-parched field — that an impoverished person had to have someone to give her water to drink, someone with access to a well or with money to use in buying water from a well. In our rain-rich land, we can understand only in a theoretical way the tradition which preserved for fifteen hundred years the memory of the feat which provided a well for this area. Not a cistern in which to collect rain water, but a spring with living water, that is, fresh water coming up out of the depths.

No, this is not a question of a special thirst; it is primarily a question concerning the conditions of life for every existing thing. And if Jesus here uses the thirst of some living thing — a plant or an animal, a man or a Samaritan woman — as a parable reflecting our longing for God, let us not immediately spiritualize it, as though it touched but one small area of our humanity, the "religious." The New Testament makes it clear that the entire creation is reaching out toward that goal for which the soul longs. There is pain in matter itself: grass and snow, birds and clouds, grazing animals and predatory beasts, man's body and soul, sigh and agonize. We read this in the Psalms: "my soul thirsts for thee;/my flesh faints for thee,/as in a dry and weary land where no water is." This does not happen apart from the thirst which can torment a man when he longs for water, or when he longs for love — to use that example too. Even the dandelion which sends its roots, like a spear, straight down to moist soil in a dry summer, is longing for God, for it longs for life, and God is the source of life. All thirst is experienced within the context of a greater thirst.

This universal longing for God can also be seen in history. This has been true not only where developments have produced patterns that we call classical, as in Jewish, Greek, and Roman history. The history of Samaria was rather checkered in nature, not at all comparable to the drama of Jewish history, or to the series of cultural achievements that characterized certain centuries in the history of Greece. The Samaritans were a mixed race; their religion was a composite, and their worship of God on Mt. Gerizim a substitute for the temple cultus in Jerusalem. But Samaritan soil thirsted for God anyway, and a cry rose up to him from out of its history: "Our fathers worshiped on this mountain . . . ."

Periodically, and in various places, a rumor has appeared to the effect that history will not have to wait until the end of time for the well of universal longing, the well of truth, the spring of reality, to be opened up to those who thirst. A

Samaritan woman had heard this too: "I know that Messiah is coming (he who is called Christ); when he comes, he will show us all things."

The stranger at the well responded with one of the *I am*s that connect the gospel of Christ with the account in Exodus of the God who spoke to Moses from the burning bush: "Say this to the people of Israel, 'I am has sent me to you.'" And with the passage in Jeremiah where Israel's God speaks of himself as a spring of fresh water.

How could this Samaritan woman, and how can we who listen to this conversation today, verify what he said? Can we bow before the prophetic insight which exposes such familiarity with the actual situation: "Go, call your husband"? That was not the only time his words penetrated the superstratum to touch upon a conflict far below. But this analytic capacity is here not the most unique thing. What is unique is the fact that this man stepped into a situation by defying accumulated contempt — contempt for a race, for a culture, for a morally tarnished individual — not in order to expose it, but in order to love the person, to love the nation. It is characteristic of Christ that he did not need to underline this unique fact. It is simply there, in the situation itself. The entire marvel is revealed in Jesus' final reply, "I who speak to you . . . ."

No one from the other side of the border had ever done that.

The source of life is, therefore, not a concept, but a person. That for which the creation in its agony reaches out is not an element such as water, fire, or air; it is the man who speaks to us here at the well, he who asked for something to drink but then forgot that *he* was thirsty. When a man loves someone, he is not satisfied with love in general, with love as a concept, with universal human love, or with love that is a surrogate for another love. There is but one person who can cause pain to cease, but one who can give peace to body and soul. So it is with creation's thirst, with the longing of body and soul; it seeks for a "you," it seeks for this man.

But doesn't it seek God? It is God who loves here at the well of Sychar, in the despised Samaria. As the water burst forth from the rock in the wilderness, so does eternity ooze out of these thirty years. Here is the rock which cracked; a cleavage in our history of pain and anguish. Here we are given what is called the gift of God.

This happened at Sychar. Where does it happen now? Jesus said: "The hour is coming when neither on this mountain nor in Jerusalem will you worship the Father." He added: "true worshipers . . . worship the Father in spirit and truth." What is "spirit and truth"? The Evangelist had just told about another conversation where it was said that "water and spirit" are the source of the new kind of life. A little later on, in the sixth chapter, it is not a spring, but five loaves and two fish that are "the gift of God," included in a message: "The words that I have spoken to you are spirit and life."

There is a meeting place that is independent of sacred times and places — such as Jerusalem or Gerizim — a meeting place where thirst is slaked: the gospel, the gospel in a word, in a fountain, in a piece of bread. For inasmuch as it is not simply our prayers which reach out for God, but the whole man and the entire creation that becomes conscious in man, so is the gospel always a piece of material reality. In the sign provided through the water and the bread an answer is given to the longing of the soil of human life, to the anguished question which our body shares in common with deserts and with arable fields.

"The gift of God" has yet another dimension. The text enables us to see for a moment how this shines forth not only in a landscape and in a chance meeting, but also in a soul. Jesus says of the one who accepts this gift: "The water that

I shall give him will become in him a spring of water . . . ."
As eternity revealed itself in the midst of our history, so can
it spring forth in the life of man, in his "innermost being," as
this is called in another passage. For when a man converses with
the gospel year after year, in word and deed, then the gospel
enters into this man. As a brook is heard to speak under the
stones and the brush piles, so is this conversation heard in a
soul's ravine far below the surface of life. "In the night also
my heart instructs me," we read in the Psalms. This inner
dialogue sometimes resembles a song of praise, but at times
it can virtually cease under a weight of unrest and anxiety, so
that a man might come to believe that it has been silenced.
But it also happens that those who feel thus go on whisper-
ing something that they themselves do not notice: "Lord, have
mercy"; "Lord Christ . . ."; "Thank you, gracious God." It is
like living by a waterfall; you never hear it because it is always there. But if the conversation is really broken off some
day because man has taken farewell of his God, then he will
experience a deathly quiet as he calls to mind how it used
to be that there actually was a dialogue in the depths of life.

Other voices can be heard on the inside as on the outside.
Temptations, greed, misgivings, satanic and human suggestions
murmur around man and within man. "How is it that you, a
Jew . . . ? Sir, you have nothing to draw with . . . . Are you
greater than our father Jacob, who gave us this well . . . ? You
say that in Jerusalem . . . ." But the voice returns, from
baptism, from the worship service, from the book, from prayer.
And this is not a series of pious opinions, theological debates,
Christian conventions. It is this man, who speaks.

Forgetfulness

Just then his disciples came. They marveled that he was talking with a woman, but none said, "What do you wish?" or, "Why are you talking with her?" So the woman left her water jar, and went away into the city, and said to the people, "Come, see a man who told me all that I ever did. Can this be the Christ?" They went out of the city and were coming to him.

Meanwhile the disciples besought him, saying, "Rabbi, eat." But he said to them, "I have food to eat of which you do not know." So the disciples said to one another, "Has any one brought him food?" Jesus said to them, "My food is to do the will of him who sent me, and to accomplish his work. Do you not say, 'There are yet four months, then comes the harvest'? I tell you, lift up your eyes, and see how the fields are already white for harvest. He who reaps receives wages, and gathers fruit for eternal life, so that sower and reaper may rejoice together. For here the saying holds true, 'One sows and another reaps.' I sent you to reap that for which you did not labor; others have labored, and you have entered into their labor."

Many Samaritans from that city believed in him because of the woman's testimony, "He told me all that I ever did." So when the Samaritans came to him, they asked him to stay with them; and he stayed there two days. And many more believed because of his word. They said to the woman, "It is no longer because of your words that we believe, for we have heard for ourselves, and we know that this is indeed the Savior of the world."

—John 4:27–42

"They marveled that he was talking with a woman." Many centuries of forgetfulness are implied in these words. Men, you see, did not discuss spiritual problems with women. Not at that time, nor for many previous ages. This was sheer forgetfulness. For God had created all of human life in his image, and had ordained a special enmity between Eve and the serpent, between the mother of men and the father of lies.

The disciples' amazement might have had another facet too. "Just think, he is talking to a Samaritan woman — the next thing to a heathen!" And one more possibility: this was a woman who came to the well in the middle of the day, when the heat was the most oppressive. Could it be that she was afraid to meet people? Did she have something to hide? Perhaps one could see what it was that she wanted to conceal: five unsuccessful attempts at marriage certainly leave their mark. And Jesus was speaking to *such* a woman.

It is still obvious, in many circles, that men prefer to sit and discuss issues by themselves, surrounded only by self-produced clouds of smoke. In our religious lives, however, one can discern the revolutionary power referred to in our text, for no one is surprised to hear that a man will discuss such problems with a woman. We now find that the liberation from a masculine monopoly has proceeded to such an extent that it is rather the men who feel embarrassed if they are surprised while conversing about religious questions.

But whatever it may be that we have been freed from, there remains a similarity between Jesus' slow-to-learn disciples and us. Now as then, among both the religious and nonreligious, we draw up definitive and obvious limits concerning the kinds of persons who can be reasonably associated with Christian interests. There is a complete list, which not only tells us what their opinions are, but also what they like to eat and drink, how they dress, and what they do to have a good time. Men forget that Jesus ever was interested in a "man of the world." Above all, they forget that Jesus never asked how sinful a man was when he chose his companions. He was only interested in knowing who needed him the most.

But the disciples of Jesus had an even harder lesson to learn that time at Sychar. It was not enough to know that their master showed an interest in a worldly-minded person. He also permitted her, such as she was, to act as a missionary. I am not suggesting that she was painted and dressed like something of a "swinger." But she had not yet cleared up the situation which Jesus pointed to when he said, "He whom you now have is not your husband." Such as she was, however, she became a pioneer. And later, when the apostles returned to this place, they had to be prepared not only to reap where she had sown, but also to look upon themselves as her co-workers.

In our day everything, even religious activity, is regulated by definitive codes. As a result, we can be sure that we know which techniques and instruments God chooses to employ. But it is unchristian for the church and the world to forget how pleased Jesus always was to ignore such prescriptions, and with a recklessness which reminds us of the tradition-defying advance of the great artists who create in colors and forms never before dreamed of.

Does a man of the world really have the right to worship Jesus? To be gripped by him, and to confess his name? Yes, if John the Evangelist is correct, we can expect a revival to begin with "secularized moderns" just as well as with the pious Christian element whose involvement in such matters is expected and self-evident. For with Christ nothing is self-evident.

It goes without saying that the woman should have hurried home with her water jar, not least because she probably had to do dishes or prepare food. It is also clear that she wanted to avoid meeting people. But she went right down the road to see the very people she had been so afraid of. And she spoke to them about the very thing she had been so afraid of discussing. "Come, see a man who told me all that I ever did." She did not try to smooth things over by saying, "He told me that he well understands all that I have done." Neither did she claim that she had become a better person. No excuses, no explanations. Just a frank and open statement of the facts: "all that I ever did."

This new attitude toward what the entire village was gossiping about clamored for an explanation. When a door once decisively — albeit ineffectively — closed has been opened, people want to know why. A powerful sensation was in the making. Soon the field was white with people — for in the East mantles are light in color.

But all the while the water jar stood there and witnessed to the fact that conventional gossip and conventional, elusive feelings of guilt had given way to a new reality. This reality was related to the confession of sin. This is not to say, by any means, that one should go around and tell everyone he meets about his sin, even though that is what happened on this occasion. The point is that the light must be permitted to shine on all things, and that the truth must be told when the situation so demands. All of the camouflage with which we try to hide our sin must be dispersed. There are many who demand this kind of reality in the novels they read but who fail to make a similar demand upon their own conscience. But wherever Christ is in the center of things, in the midst of all that is surprising and awesome, a steely desire for truth shines forth, a sober objectivity that is also associated with wonder.

This holy carelessness — when man forgets the thousands of conventions, the thousands of evasions, the thousands of petty concerns which postpone and adulterate the important ones — this holy carelessness results from an overwhelming experience, or, better yet, from an overwhelming personality.

And while the water jar stands there nonchalantly on the rim of the well, or ends up broken in pieces or standing on display in a museum somewhere, this woman of the world with her elegant clothes and her ambiguous reputation continues with her unique feminine intensity to point men to him who waits for us at the well with the water of life. "Come, see a man who told me all that I ever did. Can this be the Christ?"

Just a question. No theology. No big confession. A question. A question directed at us. It is we who must answer. Can we do that?

There was another who forgot the water jar. A few moments earlier, he had been thirsty and had asked for a drink. He was tired and hungry as well. But both hunger and thirst were forgotten after he met the woman at the well.

What else did he mean when he said, "My food is to do the will of him who sent me"? This man knew a hunger which is God's own hunger, and a thirst which is God's own thirst. Yet he was only a man off the road who came and asked for a little water. An ordinary man — so ordinary that a woman of the world ventured to speak to him about anything at all. Or did she dare do this because this man could so fully forget himself? His hunger is the hunger that loves — loves a Samaritan prostitute, a godforsaken little town, a dying thief: "I thirst."

This is the key to all of the other inexplicable facets of this passage. A heavenly longing descended into the depths and redeemed the world from below. Thus it is that the last shall be first, that what is hidden in darkness shall be lifted up into the light, that the crust of lies and habits shall be broken, that a Savior forgets all for the sake of a fellowman. And over all broods a poignant spirit of joy, as when men cut and harvest wheat.

The citizens of Sychar were not satisfied with rumors. They came out to hear and to see. They learned to know Christ. Many of us feel that we have met him. The meal that was eaten at the well continues to be served in the midst of his disciples, and when the bread is broken Christendom senses his nearness with fear and trembling. The word which supplied the water of life to a woman who had had six men continues to retain the freshness of great depths.

But nothing of this will come alive for the seeker unless it is illuminated by the holy forgetfulness displayed at Sychar, and reveals the man who came to earth with God's own hunger. If we come into his presence, we shall not bring into focus the kind of image one can dispassionately study and judge. Those who approach him are scrutinized and loved — loved in spite of everything. Then it is, probably, that they see their sins for the first time, clearly and honestly; and they do this because they see something even greater, even more reckless, even more incredible than their sins: a loving God who comes to man in the very depths of human despair. A God who is as human as Christ — for our sake. A redemption from below.

Nevertheless, what good are all our formulas and abstractions? The best sermons are not preached from pulpits. They are given by those who forget their dignity, their fragility, the goodwill they enjoy in superficial circumstances, who forget everything for that seeker among seekers who is called Christ. What I want to say is that the Lord of the harvest requires honest questioners who take with them something too great to be evaluated by a mere human assertion. Questioners who leave the door open when they go out — the door to the greatest of all perspectives. I am speaking of those men who, in the midst of all of this world's cockiness, join in the wonder expressed by the Samaritan woman: "He whom I met at the deep well — might he not be the Messiah?"

Troublesome Worshipers

> And when the time came for their purification ac-
> cording to the law of Moses, they brought him up
> to Jerusalem to present him to the Lord (as it is
> written in the law of the Lord, "Every male that
> opens the womb shall be called holy to the Lord")
> and to offer a sacrifice according to what is said in
> the law of the Lord, "a pair of turtledoves, or two
> young pigeons." Now there was a man in Jeru-
> salem, whose name was Simeon, and this man was
> righteous and devout, looking for the consolation of
> Israel, and the Holy Spirit was upon him. And it
> had been revealed to him by the Holy Spirit that
> he should not see death before he had seen the
> Lord's Christ. And inspired by the Spirit he came
> into the temple; and when the parents brought in
> the child Jesus, to do for him according to the
> custom of the law, he took him up in his arms and
> blessed God and said,
>
> "Lord, now lettest thou thy servant depart in
>   peace,
> according to thy word;
> for mine eyes have seen thy salvation
> which thou hast prepared in the presence of all
>   peoples,
> a light for revelation to the Gentiles,
> and for glory to thy people Israel."
>   —Luke 2:22–32

An old man stands in the temple, holding the child
Jesus in his arms. He thanks God for having lived to experience this day, and says that he is now ready to die, for he

has seen his Savior. Beside him stand Mary and Joseph, who have just completed the ceremonies which were customary on such occasions. Like all firstborn, Jesus belonged to the temple, and his parents have now redeemed him with five silver shekels. They have also offered two turtledoves or two young pigeons on Mary's behalf, now that she is able to go to church again after having given birth to her child. Properly speaking, it should have been a lamb, but for the poor two doves were sufficient. All of which serves to strengthen the impression that we are talking here about something very old and venerable, and to some extent also strange and curious. Some of the older ones among us may understand this, those who still remember the time when new mothers used to celebrate their return to church with a special ceremony, "the Churching of Women." But in any case no one can deny that this account is very impressive, and that the superscription rings like a church bell: Candlemas, "The Presentation of Our Lord," or "The Purification of the Blessed Virgin Mary."

But there is tension under the peaceful surface. Old Simeon was not just another worshiper. He represented an element in Jewish piety which could never be wholly bound to or tamed by the temple system — the prophetic element. When he prayed that he might be able to depart in peace, according to the words we see in the Greek text, he did not simply point to his imminent death. They refer to the discharge of duty, and the sense of relief implicit in these words suggests that this duty was not easy. The old temple service was full of signs and symbols which pointed to the Messiah; as the Letter to the Hebrews says, this was a shadow of what was to come. But no official, either in church or in state, would be content to be a shadow, and the proclamation of the coming Messiah was not popular among the priesthood in Jerusalem. It was even less so when it created political unrest and disturbed the relationship between the priesthood and the political authorities. And if it was a provocation to proclaim that the Messiah was to come, what would happen if it were asserted that he was already there? But this is what the old prophet said. And not only that — he also carried on the old prophetic tradition that burst the national boundaries of the Messianic hope by proclaiming a salvation not only for the Jews, for the priests, for religious groups, but salvation for all peoples. A light to shine for all men.

The old servant was able to depart in peace, but the child, he said, was to be "a sign that is spoken against," and of the young woman he said, "a sword will pierce through your own soul also." At that very moment, perhaps, Mary saw the fluttering doves being taken away as an offering for her, bound to her own bloodstained destiny. In the meantime, the silver shekels were being counted; thirty years later they would be paid back. Jesus would be bought back for thirty pieces of silver, then bound in the courts of the temple, condemned for blasphemy.

Thus it was that the signs shattered the pious atmosphere, and the heavenly words about salvation, light, glory became involved in earthly realities. We recall here what the Gospel of John says when Judas has gone out to earn his thirty pieces of silver: "Now is the Son of man glorified."

The ancient signs and symbols used in worship and in the sacred arts are still able today to give eloquent testimony to Jesus the Messiah. But pictures of reality can also offer refuge from reality. The prophetic message can seem to be disturbing today — even when it appears in the midst of aesthetic, theological, metaphysical signs and ideas — when it enables us to see reality itself, that which the temple officials were to make so inevitable by their attempts to do away with it. Which reality? Ask Mary how the world looked the day she finally got her son back from the prophets and the temple servants. Or ask the man on the outside, I mean the asocial person who agonized over what his deeds were worth and found an open door to the peace of which the righteous man in our text spoke so beautifully. From this point in our history, mercy aches its way through the ages. It is continually offered in the churches; it is continually surrounded by sacred signs and symbols. But if this mercy is real, and not just a mode of expression, then the entire system of concepts and rites must tremble, and the words of the prophet Malachi be fulfilled again: "The Lord whom you seek will suddenly come to his temple . . . . But who can endure the day of his coming, and who can stand when he appears?" For the reality set forth in the gospel cuts straight across all laws of custom and piety, and the man on the outside sees God's salvation. It is there that prophecy is fulfilled. The glory of Israel was revealed when the temple service was disrupted, and the light shone for the gentiles.

There are other ways in which one can take shelter from harsh realities — secular ways, as well as religious. The old man with the child in his arms can serve to illustrate a modest realm of bliss in one's own yard, a suitable election poster in a welfare society or somewhere else. And just as the temple service is not condemned in the gospel, neither is our need of happiness and security denied. Why else would Christ have been present at the wedding in Cana? Why else would he have raised the son of the widow of Nain and expressed concern, at the end, about this Mary who was his mother? But when Christ comes down the road, he demolishes the fences set up against the world. As the temple was opened for the gentiles because of him, so is the house of man opened for Lazarus and his brothers. Those places at which it is the very worst to be a man are not found on the periphery of the gospel; they form the very center of the world of Jesus Christ.

Today, prophecy stands in the midst of the temple and

throws the gates open to the world. Today, clerical garb and altar clothes are exposed to this "scouring soap." The big question is not how the church will get along over against an ungodly world; it is rather how she will fare when prophecy takes this road to the gentiles, and when that which is here consecrated to the Lord is found to be consecrated to the world. A church that is an end in itself, or that comes to serve as a sedative against dangerous prospects, a conscience-appeasing defense of the status quo — such a church is confronted today by a highly dangerous Messiah. Dangerous because he makes common cause with the kind of world such a church fears. A world whose emptiness is so great that no theology, no church music, no churchly beauty can fill it. A world which needs love enough to draw blood.

And with that we have come back to the picture we saw at the beginning — the picture of the turtledoves. For in the ancient Christian tradition the church is always identified with the Lord's mother. Because she carries this child with her through the years, it seems that she thereby verifies the bloodstained mother symbol, bound to this Messiah and his curious friends, compelled by her own mother's blood to follow him to the cross, there to give him away — away to the world. Prepared herself to die in peace, if only the light burns for the gentiles, and the glory of the cross rises up for Israel — harlots and publicans included.

There may be those who think that the church needs to hear this — or that those in the church who need to hear this are not present. But the church is coextensive with the word of God. We are all jointly responsible. And on Candlemas the Virgin Mary comes to many more than just old Simeon. Any one of us can suddenly stand there with a child in his arms — or in his soul. We can suddenly be a brother or a sister to these gentiles or to the man on the outside, suddenly unable to defend ourselves against the realities where God loves. Set on fire by the light that is to be revealed to the gentiles. Properly speaking, we all go forth responsible for a child, for God who is man. That is why the Gospel for Candlemas is so agitating, both for the one who preaches and for those who hear.

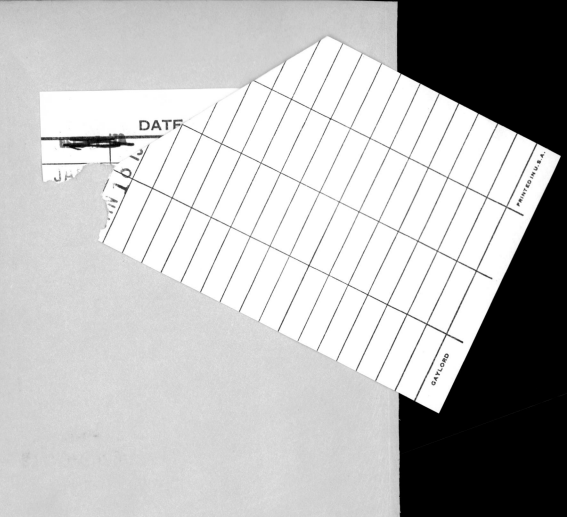

DATE

JA

GAYLORD   PRINTED IN U.S.A.